Haddad, S. K.

The principles of religion
in the Qur'an and the Bible

**G. ALLEN FLEECE LIBRARY
COLUMBIA BIBLE COLLEGE
& SEMINARY**
7435 Monticello Rd.
Columbia, SC 29203

The Principles of Religion in the Qur'an and the Bible

by
Dr. S. K. Haddad

DORRANCE PUBLISHING CO., INC.
PITTSBURGH, PENNSYLVANIA 15222

Copyright © 1992 by Dr. S. K. Haddad
All Rights Reserved
ISBN # 0-8059-3275-5
Printed in the United States of America

First Printing

Dedicated to my dear friend,
Dr. Munir Haidar

Contents

List of Abbreviations vii
Preface. ix

Chapter One:	The Need for Tolerance and Reason	1
Chapter Two:	Revelation and Inspiration	4
Chapter Three:	Principles of Interpretation	14
Chapter Four:	Human Exaggeration	30
Chapter Five:	The Alleged Sinlessness of the Prophets . .	36
Chapter Six:	The Alleged Corruption of the Bible . .	42
Chapter Seven:	Muhammad and Biblical Prophecy	46
Chapter Eight:	The Canon of the Bible	53
Chapter Nine:	The Divine Trinity	58
Chapter Ten:	The Doctrine of Man: An Exposition of the Cow 2:30-38	66
Chapter Eleven:	The Doctrine of Man Continued (The Fall) . .	75
Chapter Twelve:	The Doctrine of Man Continued (Sin) . .	86
Chapter Thirteen:	Civil Government	96
Chapter Fourteen:	Liberty	112
Chapter Fifteen:	Principles of Human Behaviour	121
Chapter Sixteen:	The Final State of Man	129
Chapter Seventeen:	The Way Back to God	137
Index:		157

List of Abbreviations

The following abbreviations are used throughout the text.

Books of The Old Testament:

Gen. (Genesis), Ex. (Exodus), Lev. (Leviticus), Num. (Numbers), Deut. (Deuteronomy), Josh. (Joshua), Jud. (Judges), 1&2 Sam. (1&2 Samuel), 1&2 Ki. (1&2 Kings), 1&2 Chr. (1&2 Chronicles), Ezr. (Ezra), Neh. (Nehemiah), Ps. (Psalms), Pr. (Proverbs), Is. (Isaiah), Jer. (Jeremiah), Ezek. (Ezekiel), Dan. (Daniel), Hos. (Hosea), Hab. (Habakuk), Zech. (Zechariah), Mal. (Malachi).

Books Of The New Testament:

Mt. (Matthew), Mk. (Mark), Lk. (Luke), Jn. (John), Ro. (Romans), 1&2 Cor. (1&2 Corinthians), Gal. (Galatians), Eph. (Ephesians), Phil. (Philippians), Col. (Colossians), 1&2 Thess. (1&2 Thessalonians), 1&2 Tim. (1&2 Timothy), Tit. (Titus), Phm. (Philemon), Heb. (Hebrews), Jas. (James), 1&2 Pet. (1&2 Peter), 1 Jn. (1 John), Rev. (Revelation).

Others:

Qur'anic references according to number of Surah and verse: 2:30 means Surah 2, verse, 30; Barn. (Gospel of Barnabas); v. (verse), vv. (verses).

Preface

This book aims to discuss the doctrines of God and man from the Qur'anic and Biblical perspectives. It is not concerned with denominational beliefs. The *Qur'an* and *Bible* are treated with the respect and authority which Muslims and Christians, respectively, attach to them. No attempt is made to prove or disprove either book. Much of the argument is based upon the *Qur'an* in an effort to explain to Muslims that the *Qur'an*, like the *Bible*, should be interpreted by what it says and not by means of extraneous tradition.

The Qur'anic quotations are from Arthur J. Arberry's translation (*The Koran*, Oxford University Press), with corrections where necessary to bring it closer to the Arabic text. The Biblical quotations are from the Authorized Version, with modernization of relevant words.

Chapter One
The Need for Tolerance and Reason

It is inevitable that the religions of the world should disagree in matters of doctrine and practice. Christianity and Islam are missionary religions. They strive to convert men to their way. Religion's main function is to bring God and man together. This life is preparatory for the next. Most people, including the religious, are concerned with temporal rather than eternal issues. They think that ritual has a role in vital issues. What does it matter if you stand or kneel or prostrate yourself when you pray, as long as your heart is right with God? Does the length of your robe or what you wear on your head effect your eternal destiny? True religion is disregarded while men fight for the unimportant.

INTOLERANCE

When two men disagree, is it right for them to exterminate each other? Is there no recourse to reason and understanding? If conflict is the answer, then we are at the level of the jungle beasts that fight over remnants of their prey.

The Biblical doctrine of the Trinity is blasphemous with reference to the *Qur'an*. The denial of the divinity of Christ and the Holy Spirit is blasphemous with reference to the *Bible*. Is the answer to be found in a conflict of fists and weapons? When two men fight for different viewpoints, the winner proves that he is physically stronger than his opponent. The rightness of his case remains undetermined. Convince me of the unreasonableness of my case, or I will convince you of its reasonableness. Men destroy what they fear. Should this be their attitude in the variety of their beliefs? Truth must determine the matter between conflicting ideas. Prejudice is the scorpion of the mind, and fear of the truth the head in the sand.

As instituted religions, Christianity and Islam denied God when they subjugated people by force. They preached a merciful God while their swords struck the necks of unbelievers. Oppression, fear and torture are contrary to a holy cause. How can coercion and subjugation be the instruments of peace? By what right does a man control the mind of another who has a God-given ability to think? Islam spread its influence by military power, despite the Muslims' denial of this fact. When Christianity became respectable in the fourth century as the legal religion of the Roman Empire, it lost much of its true spirit. The Visigothic Arians of the sixth century, who denied the divinity of Christ, persecuted the orthodox Catholic bishops. The Monotheletes, who believed in the one divine will of Christ, were the persecutors of the seventh century. The eighth century saw the persecution of those who believed in holy images by those who refused such worship. The church instigated the unholy Crusades against the Muslims in the Middle Ages. That same church was also the instrument of terror and injustice which tortured and executed, through the Inquisition, those who did not subscribe to its whims and fancies. No neck was safe. The innocent lost their lives on trumped-up charges of heresy. There was no freedom of thought and, consequently, no individual freedom. It was the case of master and slave, the strong crushing the weak. The Reformation was followed by religious wars. Protestants and Roman Catholics massacred one another. Men were burnt at the stake in seventeenth-century Oxford and London. This was done in God's name. When man slaughters his fellow man to defend a helpless God, he makes him the reason for his wickedness. More cruelty was done by the so-called followers of God than by the sword of Atilla the Hun, or the Mongolian hordes of Ghengis Khan. The patience of God defies understanding.

DICTATORSHIP

Dictatorship is found not only in the political realm but also in the home, the church and the mosque. It is religious dictatorship that concerns us. Men of religion regard themselves the spokesmen of God who should be offered blind obedience and never questioned. This is not to decry the authority which God gives to his ministers. The aim is to deny the dictatorship over the minds of men which many think is their right.

Man loves to tread down his fellow while he wears the robe of hypocritical humility. The greatest evil is when men and women are denied the worship of God according to their conscience. God's authority is usurped by those who think themselves to be the guardians of the conscience. Religious men tend to be fanatics. They show less tolerance than unbelievers. Their arrogance betrays a mind shackled by its own notions of good and evil. This is the basis of religious persecution, and it leaves little room for common sense and reason. Men become unbending and unwilling to listen to another. They betray a hidden fear of reason. Islam is more blameworthy than Christianity in this regard. A man may adopt or remain in Islam, but may not leave it without peril to his life. Jesus said: "Whosoever therefore shall humble himself as this little child, the same is the greatest in the kingdom of heaven," but "Whoso shall offend one of these little ones who believe in me, it were better for him that a millstone were hanged about his neck, and he were drowned in the depth of the sea" (Mt.18:4-6). Freedom of faith must be allowed even to a little child. Without it, man faces the wrath of the Almighty.

Chapter Two

Revelation and Inspiration

God is infinite and unsearchable. He lives in the fullness of his being, and from eternity is the same. He is abundant life, giving life to others. He created the angels then man. Man was not created for his own pleasure, to live in a garden and enjoy himself. He was to be the friend of God. If the angels lived in God's presence, how much more was Adam to be, having been created better than the angels according to the *Qur'an?* (2:34). For this reason man was given a personality that could respond to the personality of God. God lowered himself to the level of his creature. He was not to be a friend from a distance. The friendship was to be of kindred spirits. When man disobeyed God, he was banished from his presence. Sin could not live with God. In order for man to return to his former relationship with God, the offending cause must be removed and man's nature must be restored. God, in his mercy, provided for the restoration of man. The object of revelation after Adam's fall had one major purpose: the restoration, or rather the redemption of man.

THE NEED FOR A RECORD OF REVELATION

A record of revelation was necessary when writing was invented. The events of God's dealing with men would be passed from generation to generation. Christ told John to write what he saw (Rev.1:11). The urgency of a record was noted early in the history of Islam when many of those who memorized the *Qur'an* were killed in battle. The *Bible* is a record of progressive historical revelation compiled over the passage of centuries. God safeguarded the knowledge of his dealings with men by inspiring men to write his word. This is the basis of the authority of the *Bible*. The *Qur'an* was right to acknowledge the *Torah*, the *Gospel*, the *Psalms*, and other scriptures which the Jews possessed.

Revelation could not endure its verbal transmission without becoming corrupted. An item of news changes rapidly from its original version when it is retold. The Semitic inhabitants of ancient Iraq provide an example of what man did with revelation when he was left to himself. Adam knew the One God, but the knowledge deteriorated into polytheism; man was then the servant, not the friend, of the gods. The story of the flood was distorted, as seen in the epic of Gilgamish. It was mixed up with the tales of the gods who differed in their views of what to do with man. Gilgamish's quest for immortality failed. No plan of redemption was considered. This is in marked contrast with the Biblical account. It is a fallacy to find the origin of the Biblical creation and flood narratives in Mesopotamian myths.

THE NATURE OF REVELATION

Revelation is general and special.

General Revelation

General revelation is through the natural world and the conscience. "And of his signs is the creation of the heavens and the earth and the creeping things he scattered abroad in them." (42:29). "These are signs for a people that have understanding" (2:164). "It is he who made the sun a radiance and the moon a light and determined it by stations, that you might know the number of the years and the reckoning. God has not created that except by the truth, distinguishing the signs to a people who know. In the alternation of the night and day and what God has created in the heavens and the earth, surely are signs for a godfearing people" (10:5,6). The *Bible* has the same message: "The heavens declare the glory of God and the firmament shows his handiwork. Day unto day utters speech and night unto night shows knowledge. There is no speech or language where their voice is not heard" (Ps.19:1-3). The universe should drive people to faith in God. Paul shows the condemnation of those who do not believe, "for the invisible things from the creation of the world are clearly seen, being understood by the things that are made, even his eternal power and Godhead: so that they are without excuse" (Ro.1:20). Astronomers may study the depths of the universe and refuse to believe in the One who made it. They are without excuse.

General revelation is deficient. The sun, the rain and the produce of the earth tell of a benevolent God. But the cruelty of nature—in the animal world, and in hurricanes, earthquakes, raging seas, floods, drought, famine, starvation—may lead many to conclude that God is cruel.

General revelation is also through the conscience. God implanted the law of nature into man's heart. He can differentiate between right and wrong and his actions are judged by his conscience (Ro. 2:14,15). Man may deny God and still his own conscience, but it cries out for help in times of danger and at the moment of death.

Special Revelation

Special revelation is through the direct dealings between God and man, as embodied in the sacred books. It serves to control evil in this world, and to prepare man for his eternal destiny.

THE METHODS OF REVELATION

Audible Speech

Muhammad heard the angel Gabriel say to him, "Read in the name of your Lord who created" (96:1-5). The revelation persisted in audible and visual forms. It was often prefaced by the word "say," that is, tell God's word which you hear. Audible words were heard only by the intended listener. Saul of Tarsus, who later became known as the apostle Paul, saw the risen Christ and heard him. Those who were with him heard only a sound (Acts 9:7; 22:9). When Jesus prayed and the Father answered, the people "said that it thundered: others said, an angel spoke to him" (Jn.12:29). "God spoke to Moses by speaking" (4:164). He "called him out of the midst of the bush and said, Moses, Moses" (Ex.3:4). When God gave the commandments to the children of Israel, they were accompanied by thunder and lightning and the noise of a trumpet so that they said to Moses, "You speak with us and we will hear: let not God speak with us, lest we die" (Ex.20:19). Even Nebuchadnezzar heard "a voice from heaven saying, O King Nebuchadnezzar, to you it is spoken: the kingdom is departed from you" (Dan. 4:31).

The *Qur'an* represents the exact words of the angel to Muhammad, words which came in a piecemeal fashion as the occasion demanded. This type of revelation was mechanical, where the hearer had the job of delivering what he heard, whether he understood the message or not. He was like a postman, or like the pen with which a message is written. Muhammad understood all that was said to him. If his opponents understood his words and disliked them, was he less than they? All the prophets understood the message to the people of their day. Jonah even refused to go at first. But when the prophets of Israel prophesied of Christ, their understanding was incomplete. Isaiah prophesied (chapter 53) of the suffering servant of the Lord who was to die for others yet see the fruit which his death would produce. Peter said that these prophesies were given by the Holy Spirit for the benefit of those who heard the gospel (1Pet.1:10-12).

Dreams

Abraham said, "My son, I see in my sleep that I sacrifice you" (37:102). Joseph and Daniel were interpreters of dreams (12:36-49; Gen.40 & 41; Dan.1:17; 5:12). The events in Joseph's life commenced with a dream (12:4; Gen.37:9). God spoke in dreams to Jacob (Gen.28:12; 31:11), Solomon (1Ki.3:5), and to Joseph the husband of Mary and to the wise men (Mt.1:20; 2:12-22).

Visions

Visions may be associated with an alteration of consciousness or not. The *Hadith*, or traditions of Muhammad, tells how revelation came to him.[1,2] It was at first in dreams. After six months he saw the angel, but was uncertain of his identity. The angel said, "Read," and he answered, "I am not reading." He felt as if he was being strangled or embraced tightly, and he trembled in the coldness of his sweat. He returned to his wife Khadijah saying, "Wrap me up, wrap me up." He later saw the angel sitting on a throne between heaven and earth. He was aware. "He saw him poised being on a higher horizon . . . then revealed to his servant what he revealed" (53:2-18). At times he would swoon as sweat dripped from his brow and his tongue moved hastily,[3] or the colour of his face changed and his head drooped. "Do not move your tongue to hasten it: ours is to gather it and to recite it" (75:16-19). It appears that Muhammad experienced both types of vision.

God came to Abraham in visions (Gen.15), and also to Jacob (Gen.46:2). Balaam was in a trance with his eyes open (Num.24:4). God spoke by visions to the prophets of Israel, and needed to explain some to Daniel (Dan.7-11). Even the false prophets claimed to see visions, and God condemned them for their lies (Jer.14:14; 23:16).

The Condescension of God

When Aaron and Miriam spoke ill of Moses, God said: "If there be a prophet among you, I the Lord will make myself known to him in a vision, and will speak to him in a dream. My servant Moses is not so, who is faithful in all my house. With him I will speak mouth to mouth, even apparently, and not in dark speeches; and the similitude of God shall he behold" (Num.12:6-8). The word similitude, or likeness, helps to explain another method of revelation.

Moses said to God: "I beseech you, show me your glory." God answered, "You cannot see my face, for there shall no man see me and live" (Ex.33:18-20). "My Lord, show me that I behold you. He said you shall not see me" (7:143). When Gideon and the parents of Samson saw an angel of the Lord, they thought they would die (Jud.6:22; 13:22). God is too holy to be seen as he is by sinful man. But will he not reveal himself in a veiled manner? Is not man the highest form of his creation? Can he not appear as man? The object of revelation was that he should make himself known. It is wrong to think that he remained distant. His appearances in human form are called theophanies.

Messengers came as men from God to Abraham (11:69-76). He feared them when they refused to eat. They reassured him. The Biblical account says that they did eat (Gen.18:8). If they could speak with tongues, lungs and vocal chords, could they not eat? They told Abraham that Sarah would bear Isaac, and they were going to the people of Lot. Abraham knew that judgment was imminent. He wanted to save Lot, so he asked God to relent from his purpose. "So when the awe departed and the good tidings came to him, he was arguing (disputing) with us concerning the people of Lot" (11:75). The *Qur'an* is never in doubt whether God is speaking of himself, of another, or through another. "He was disputing with *us*" means that Abraham disputed with God, who came as a messenger. The Biblical version is similar. "They said to him, where is Sarah your wife? He said, behold in the tent, and he said, I will certainly return to you" (Gen.18:9,10). "And the Lord said, shall I hide from Abraham the thing I do?" "And the men turned their faces from thence and went toward Sodom: but Abraham stood before the Lord" (Gen.18:17-23). "The men," "I," and "the Lord" are used interchangeably for God, in these passages. If God used "I" all the time, Abraham may have thought that he saw God as he is. The *Bible* says the men were three; the *Qur'an* uses the plural of more than two to describe them. God came as a man: He talked and ate with Abraham, whom he called his friend (4:125; 2Chr.20:7; Jas.2:23). Friendship implies a personal relationship, and not remoteness.

When Adam and his wife sinned, "their Lord called to them" (7:22) as if from a distance. Moses saw the similitude of God, not God as he is. "God spoke to Moses by speaking" (4:164). "The Lord spoke to Moses face to face as a man speaks to his friend" (Ex.33:11). This means he spoke directly to him. He made his voice and speech comprehensible. He did not elevate Moses to heaven, but came down to his level at the mountain. If you say that God is too great to come down to man's level, then he is too great to speak with him. Deny his condescension and you deny God his grace and mercy by restraining his power and wisdom.

What did Moses hear? Was it God's voice in God's language? Did God use the language of Egypt or Midian or Syria, with their intermixing of words and dialects? Whatever it was, God humbled himself to speak the language, dialect and accent of Moses, in a man's voice. Hidden behind the form of his appearance was God the Almighty Spirit who cannot be seen by sinful man. Had Moses not felt at ease with God, he would not have asked to see him as he is. God did not reprimand him for his request.

The Angel of the Lord

When Hagar ran away from Sarah, "the angel of the Lord found her by a fountain of water in the wilderness." He said to her, "Return to your mistress . . . I will multiply your seed exceedingly" (Gen.16:7-11). We see again the "I" and "the Lord" side by side. The same pattern is seen when Hagar was finally cast out (Gen.21:17,18), and when the angel of the Lord stopped Abraham from slaying his son: "I know that you fear God seeing you have not withheld your son, your only son from me" (Gen.22:12). The angel is identified with God.

Muslims criticize the story of Jacob's struggle with the angel as being untrue (Gen.32:24-32). "And Jacob was left alone; and there struggled a man with him until the breaking of the day." Jacob remembered the incident when he blessed Joseph's sons: "The Angel who redeemed me from evil, bless the lads" (Gen.48:16). Hosea said: "He had power over the angel and prevailed: he wept and made supplication to him" (Hos.12:4). Jacob's brother, Esau, came against him with 400 men (Gen.32:6). Jacob had received his father's patriarchal blessing in place of his brother. He was now willing to lose all his possessions to save his family. God showed him that if Jacob prevailed against him in a struggle, would he not prevail against his brother? God's mercy was incomparable in demonstrating with an action what words could never convey.

Will you be surprised to know that the *Qur'an* refers indirectly to the event? "All food was lawful to the children of Israel except what Israel forbade himself before the *Torah* was sent down" (3:93). Jacob is called

Israel in the *Qur'an* one other time, with regard to the prophets who were of his seed (19:58). He is otherwise invariably called Jacob.

The name Israel was given to Jacob on the occasion of his wrestling with the angel. "Your name shall be called no more Jacob, but Israel, for as a prince you have power with God and with men and have prevailed" (Gen.32:28). This is the first link with 3:93 that calls Jacob Israel. The second link is with respect to food. "And the hollow of Jacob's thigh was strained as he wrestled with him," "therefore the children of Israel eat not of the sinew which shrank" (Gen.32:25,32). "All food was lawful except what Israel forbade himself," falls into this context. The *Bible* describes in detail what the *Qur'an* summarizes in one verse.

The angel of the Lord differed from all other angels in having the right to speak as God. He said to Abraham, I know that you have not kept your son from me, and to Hagar, I will bless the lad and I will make him a great nation. He preserved Jacob's life, the holder of the covenant, of whose seed the nations of the earth will be blessed. The angel of the Lord is the angel of the covenant: "Behold, I will send my messenger and he shall prepare the way before me and the Lord whom you seek shall suddenly come to his temple, even the messenger of the covenant" (Mal.3:1). The prophecy referred to Christ as the messenger or angel of the covenant, and to John (Yahya) as the messenger who prepared his way (Lk.1:17; Jn.1:23). Stephen said that Christ was the angel who spoke to Moses on Mount Sinai (Acts7:37,38). Christ is therefore the angel of the Lord who spoke as God. It is significant that Abraham and Jacob built an altar where the angel of the Lord appeared to them. They recognized him as God (Gen.12:7,8; 28:10-22; 35:1).

Incarnation

There is a great difference between knowing about a person and knowing that person. The same applies to the knowledge of God. Having condescended to speak and appear to men, veiled in the form of a man, he finally appeared in the person of Jesus Christ as true man. This was inevitable since the object of revelation was for God to make himself known to man in a plan of restoration.

The incarnation does not mean that Jesus, a man, became God, but that God became man as he entered the swamp to save man. God completed his revelation through the incarnation.

God will be seen by all on the judgment day. Muhammad is said to have gone up to heaven. Some say that he saw God.[4,5] If man could enter heaven and see God, would not God come down to the level of men?

The incarnation marked the limit or extent of revelation. Revelation after Adam's sin started in the garden: "And Adam received words from his Lord" (2:37). The Biblical account spoke of the woman's seed who would crush the devil's head (Gen.3:15). He was Mary's son, Jesus. The *Bible* has a unified message concerning him. There was no other way to redeem mankind from its condition of sin. If Adam failed to offer obedience in his state of innocence, who of his progeny is able to restore himself by his own prowess to that original state? Revelation was finalized in the work of the redeemer.

INSPIRATION

Inspiration is the influence of God's Spirit upon the mind so that it writes God's words, which can bring men to God. A vision seen, if recorded, has to be written by inspiration so that the record is accurate. Moses needed inspiration to write down the details of the ark which he saw on the mountain. The exercise of the human mind without the Spirit could not be without error. The mind of the writer remained free. This explains why the versions of the *Gospel* differ; each has the imprint and style of its writer. There was no mechanical element. Each wrote according to his talent and ability. The same applies to the other books of the *Bible*. The shepherd Amos wrote as a shepherd. Peter was not as learned as Paul, so his arguments were not as profound. Isaiah wrote of the burden of the Lord when he prophesied the fate of the nations. But when he spoke of the redemption which God provided in Christ, he burst forth in a most magnificent style of prose and poetry; many attribute Chapters 40-66 to another man. This aspect of the *Bible*, its humanity, is a proof of its divine origin. It is not of one style, as brought forth from a mould. If men invented its content they would have tried to unify its style. Its amazing unity, despite its diversity, is found in its central message about Christ. "All scripture is given by inspiration of God" (2 Tim.3:16). "Holy men of God spoke as they were moved by the Spirit of God" (2 Pet.1:21). It is as if the Spirit wrote the text with the active help of the writers.

THE NECESSITY OF A NATION OF GOD'S PEOPLE

God promised a redeemer. He chose that, of Abraham's seed, all the families of the earth would be blessed (Gen.12:3; 22:18). He repeated the promise to Isaac (Gen.26:4) and Jacob (Gen.28:14). Judah was then chosen (Gen. 49:10) and, of his seed, David (2 Sam.7:16; 23:5) and Christ (Ps.110; 45:6,7). The *Qur'an* places Joseph in the same line: "So your Lord will choose you and teach you the interpretation of tales and perfect his favour upon you and upon the house of Jacob as he perfected it formerly to your fathers, Abraham and Isaac" (12:6). The *Bible* is right in placing Judah and not Joseph in the line of blessing, for of him came David and Christ. From Judah onwards, the promise took the form of an everlasting kingdom.

If God had not chosen a people and gathered them in a particular land, the coming of Christ would have been lost to the world. He would have come unannounced and no one would have known who he was. His cause would have been lost in the tumult of humanity. For this reason the people were trained by the prophets to expect the coming of the Messiah. The whole nation was geared for the event. When John came, they asked him, "Who are you?" and he confessed, "I am not the Christ" (Jn.1:19,20). The *Qur'an* agrees that the people of Israel were chosen: "Children of Israel, remember my favour wherewith I favoured you and fulfil my covenant and I shall fulfil your covenant" (2:40). "I have preferred you above all beings" (2:47). He gave them the promised land and Moses said: "O my people, enter the holy land which God has written for you and turn not back in your traces" (5:20-36). The choosing of the children of Israel was the means by which Christ was to come of Abraham. His advent had to be unmistakable. God accomplished the purpose for which he chose the people and the land when Christ came. As revelation ended in Christ, so the role of the children of Israel as the people of God's choice ended. They were replaced by a spiritual people, the believers in Christ, called the new Israel of God (Ro.9:6; Gal.6:16).

Summary

True religion is not the aspiration of man to know God, but the condescension of God to redeem fallen man. All was well when Adam kept his integrity. When he disobeyed, he was sent out of the presence of God. God took the initiative as an act of mercy and guided him by revelation. He revealed himself to the prophets through dreams and visions and spoke to Moses directly, in his own language and accent. This was one step removed from his appearance as a man and, ultimately, in the person of Jesus Christ. It was inevitable since God wanted to be known. In order to effect man's restoration through history, God had to enter history. This was not by compulsion, but of his good pleasure. If God bothered to make man out of clay and breathe into him the life of his Spirit, he would surely come down to man's level and reveal himself effectively. God had to remove the barriers that stood in the way of reconciliation. There was no way out of the incarnation after God decided to save. It was a necessity if the restoration of man was to take place. Muhammad saw God, according to Islamic tradition.[6] Men see him on the Judgment Day. Should they not have seen him as he humbled himself to save them on a hill outside Jerusalem?

References

1. Sahih ul-Bukhari (Dar uj-jeel, Beirut), vol.1, pp.1-3; vol.6, pp.214, 215.
2. Ibn Sa'ad, Attabakat ul-kubra, (Dar Sader, Beirut) vol.1, pp.194-199.
3. Ibn Sa'ad, Ibid. vol.1, p.198.
4. Al-Bukhari, Ibid. vol.1, pp.97, 98.
5. Ibn Sa'ad, Ibid. vol.1, p.213.
6. Al-Bukhari. Ibid. vol.6, p.56.

Chapter Three

Principles of Interpretation

Although the prophets preached to their own generation, their message was for all generations. Interpretation of the *Qur'an* and the *Bible* must be governed by the same principles which apply to the interpretation of any statement or thesis written by men. The cardinal principle is that God spoke in human language.

GOD USED THE LANGUAGE OF MEN

Some have suggested that God spoke to all the prophets in Arabic. This is denied by the *Qur'an*: "We have sent no messenger save with the tongue of his people" (14:4). The essential point is that the words expressed the purpose of God and the meaning of God. He who understands the language and follows sound rules should be able to understand the meaning of God. Interpretation should not be reserved for scholars or men of religion. Those claiming special authority are usurpers of men's minds. When Muhammad called men to repentance, he expected them to understand the message. He did not say, come tomorrow and I will explain to you what I said today. The prophets discoursed with their listeners, who were either pleased or offended. As long as we allow for changes in the language and its usage over the years, comprehension should be possible. It is recorded of Jesus that "the common people heard him gladly" (Mk.12:37). He interpreted some of his parables for his disciples when they did not understand. No priest, pope, or Imam has the right to monopolize the scriptures and consider that he alone is the interpreter of God. This is not to deny the wisdom of the scholars, but the learned differ in their interpretations in the Christian and Muslim camps. Who is to judge what is true? One must weigh and consider the evidence.

LITERAL INTERPRETATION AND THE ROLE OF THE FIGURATIVE

Literal interpretation takes words to mean exactly what they say: "take off your shoes" does not mean "purify yourself." Moses took off his shoes in response to the command. He did not wash himself or comb his beard and hair. He understood the command literally.

Figurative interpretation allows for metaphors and images in speech. It leaves room for the spiritualization of meaning where intended. When God says, "cleanse your hearts and not your garments," he does not mean that you should go to the surgeon and ask him to take your heart out and wash it. Nor does it mean that you should not wash your clothes and go about dirty and stinking. It means that God does not want a superficial, ritualistic obedience, but a pure conscience towards him.

Those who regard the story of Adam as a myth are forever groping in darkness, unable to understand the state of the world. The historical reality of the Qur'anic and Biblical narratives is emphasized when it is linked with the story of the creation. If Adam was a myth, so was the creation. The mythologists regard the narratives as extracts of confused Mesopotamian tales. The events were real, but men corrupted the truth over the years and linked it with the myths of their gods. The writers of the scriptures were inspired to write events as they really happened.

A literal interpretation is the only one that explains the problem of evil: that God did not create a world which festered with sin. The concept of Adam's literal fall is essential to an understanding of the world. Politicians, economists, moralists, socialists, philosophers, and all manner of idealists, are at a loss in the management of the affairs of men because they do not recognize the principle of sin.

Certain passages of the *Bible* do not support literal interpretation. The context leaves no doubt of the intended meaning. When Christ said of the bread, "this is my body," and of the cup, "this cup is the new testament in my blood" (Lk.22:19,20), he spoke figuratively. He did not mean that the bread and wine changed into his body and blood as the Roman Catholic Church believes. Christ did not institute cannibalism.

APOCALYPTIC LANGUAGE

The *Bible* contains passages that are rich in symbolism. They have been a trap for loose-thinking Christians. The book of Revelation is the prime example. It has been interpreted without any consideration that it was written to comfort first-century Christians who were suffering persecution. It tells them that Christ is the conqueror of all their enemies. What is the use of telling them what they could never understand, of wars of horrific proportions fought with nuclear weapons and the like? It takes a blind man not to see that the return of Christ is linked in the *Bible* with the Judgment Day and the end of time.

The Day of the Lord serves as an example of apocalyptic language. It is described in prophetic symbolism as a day of wrath, judgment, or salvation. "And I will show wonders in the heavens and in the earth: blood and fire and pillars of smoke. The sun shall be turned into darkness and the moon into blood before the great and terrible Day of the Lord comes" (Joel 2:28-32; Acts 2:17-21). Peter applied the prophecy to the coming of the Holy Spirit upon the church. The blood and darkness and other descriptions drew attention to a most striking and unique event in the history of the world.

IMAGERY

Muslims have criticized the *Bible* for likening God with things lesser than himself. He is the rock, the shield and the fortress of his people. The terms describe his steadfastness, immutability, guardianship and protection. "As an eagle stirs up her nest, flutters over her young, spreads abroad her wings, takes them, bears them on her wings: so the Lord alone did lead him" (Deut.32:11,12). The tenderness of God to his people is expressed.

The *Qur'an* employs imagery of God. "God is the light of the heavens and earth: the likeness of his light is as a niche wherein is a lamp, the lamp in a glass, the glass as if it is a planet of pearls, kindled from a blessed tree" (24:35). The verse employs seven images. It does not mean that God has the physical properties of light and that his light is sustained by an almost shining olive tree. The description is of his glorious majesty in terms which we can understand. That God "has the keys of heaven and earth" (39:63; 42:12), does not mean that heaven has gates and God is the doorman who carries a bunch of keys. The meaning is that he blesses the earth or withholds his blessing.

ANTHROPOMORPHISM

By this is meant that human form and personality are attributed to God. It is not meant that he possesses human form. Yet who knows that he does not? We cannot comprehend him, who is Spirit, without such terms. When the *Qur'an* says that after the creation God settled upon the throne (7:54; 13:2), it does not mean that he has a physical structure that enabled him to sit as does a man, or dangle his legs in the air. He is said to have hands: "Have they not seen that we created what our hand made?" (36:71). The kingdom is in his hands, and the wind (23:88; 7:57; 27:63). It is not meant that God has fingers and a thumb, but that he controls and rules over all things. He hears the cry of the oppressed, and sees their trouble and knows their sorrow. The *Hadith* speaks of his right hand, ears, face and that he will bare his leg.[1]

Apart from descriptions arising from human form, the *Qur'an* and the *Bible* describe God as possessing a personality which responds to events and has feelings. Muslims criticize Gen 6:6, which says: "It repented the Lord that he made man on the earth and it grieved him at his heart." They ask how God can create man, then regret his action. They miss the point. The context describes the magnitude of evil into which man had sunk, so that it became necessary to destroy him with a flood. Had God been a man, he would have regretted making man. This emphasizes the terrible state of man in sin. God was not taken by surprise, for he knew what man would do. The verse asserts the extent of man's vileness in a most positive way. There is no eloquence in the world that can describe the situation better. The verse also shows God's tenderness towards his creatures. He had to destroy them, yet he did not enjoy seeing them die. "As I live, says the Lord, I have no pleasure in the death of the wicked, but that the wicked turn from his ways and live: turn ye, turn ye from your evil ways; for why will you die, O house of Israel?" (Ezek.33:11). This is how God pleads with sinners to escape disaster.

"God is a consuming fire, even a jealous God" (Deut.4:24) means that as a raging fire he consumes his enemies, and that as a jealous husband he will not share the love of his people with another. Do you think that God is impassionate and cold? He who gave feelings to man, does he not feel? He loves, shows mercy and kindness but also shows anger and takes vengeance (4:93; 5:95). He derides and curses evildoers (2:15; 4:46) and devises more cunningly than the cunning (3:54). He takes the wise in their own craftiness (Job 5:13) and turns again, or repents towards believers (33:73).

If someone asks you who created the world you answer, "God did." He asks, "How?" You say, "He spoke and it was done." He asks, "Does he have the anatomical features for speech?" You say, "No, he spoke in his mind." He says, "You speak audibly; is your creator dumb? Is his mind of nervous tissue?" You say, "God is Spirit." He says, "You mean a ghost?" You say, "No, he is shapeless." He says "Is there anything shapeless on earth?" And so you find yourself unable to express the description of God without using human terms.

THE CONTEXT

Nothing is worse than taking verses at their face value, without considering their context. When Jesus said, "my Father is greater than I" (Jn.14:28), he spoke as a man about to die on the cross. He did not refer to his position in eternity where he is equal with the Father.

THE HISTORICAL BACKGROUND

The command to destroy the people of Canaan is a disturbing part of Biblical history to Muslims and Christians alike. God told Abraham that he would bring his seed out of bondage (in Egypt) at the proper time "for the iniquity of the Amorites is not yet full" (Gen.15:16). The Amorites lived in the hill country in the fourteenth century B.C., when the children of Israel entered (Num.13:29). They occupied Syria and Palestine in about 2,000 B.C. or earlier. The Mediterranean Sea was known as the Sea of Amurru after them. About 1850 B.C., in Abraham's day, the Amorites were regarded as representing the people of Canaan. They had to work the full measure of iniquity. Their iniquity was the sacrifice of their children by fire to their gods. The children of Israel were the rod of anger of the Almighty against them, forbidden to send their children through the fire to Molech (Lev.18:21; 20:2-5; Deut.18:10). Ahab, king of Judah, and also Manassah practised this evil. He "made his son to pass through the fire, according to the abominations of the heathen, whom the Lord cast out before the children of Israel" (2 Ki.16:3; 21:2-6). The verse, with Deut. 20:17,18, suggests this was the major reason for which the Lord cast out the heathen. The *Bible* contains its own history for interpretation.

QUR'ANIC ABROGATION

Abrogation is the process whereby one verse replaces another and makes it redundant. Muhammad was accused of forgetting verses and changing his instructions to his followers. The verses came in reply: "We do not abrogate or cause a verse to be forgotten, but to bring the better or the like of it" (2:106). "And when we exchange a verse in the place of a verse, and God knows very well what he sends down, they say, you are a mere forger; but most of them do not know" (16:101).

"Many of the people of the Book wish that they might restore you as unbelievers after you have believed, in the jealousy of their souls, after the truth has become clear to them, but forgive and pardon until God brings his command" (2:109). The Arab commentators explain how the prominent Jews of Madinah opposed Muhammad. Some mocked after the battle of Uhud in 625 A.D., when the Muslims received a hard blow.[2,3]

The abrogating verse came in 631: "Fight those who do not believe in God or in the Last Day and do not forbid what God and his messenger have forbidden and do not practice the religion of truth, of those to whom the Book was given until they pay tribute out of hand having been humiliated" (9:29). Muhammad had vanquished Arabia by 631 and was preparing for the invasion of Syria. Tolerance was replaced by a command to fight within six years, indicating that Islam was to be a militant religion when it became able to carry out its role.

Wine drinking provides another example of abrogation. The *Qur'an* said at first: "It contains a heinous sin and benefits for men" (2:219). It could be used for its benefits. The next injunction said, "Do not draw near to prayer when you are drunk" (4:43). The final word abolished wine as an abomination and one of the works of Satan (5:90,91). A drunken Muslim spoke inadvisedly of others in the Muslim camp, or killed another's camel.[4,5] 'Umar ibn el-Khattab is said to have prayed for a clear answer about the matter, and the prohibition came. The abrogation came in a short period of time, as if God had not made up his mind. But if the experience was to show Muslims the evil of wine, then its purpose was fulfilled. Drunkenness almost led to an armed conflict between Muslims.

CONSISTENCY

Contradiction must be avoided, unless it is truly present.

Statements of Fact

A statement of fact does not indicate that a cardinal doctrine is being established. When a reporter writes about a crime, it does not mean that he condones the crime. Muslims have accused the *Bible* of teaching incest. Lot's daughters made him drunk and committed incest with him (Gen.19:30-38). The *Bible* does not say "Well done, daughters of Lot." It reports what happened. If the *Bible* was fabricated by men, they would have hidden the faults of the great.

Parallelism

The *Bible* has been unjustly accused of contradiction because of its parallel passages. Parallelism enriches the record of revelation. The *Qur'an* employs this technique as well. Adam's case will illustrate the point. Comparison of 2:34-38 with 20:116-126 shows that the passages use different details in describing Adam's fall. God told Adam that Satan was his enemy and described life's hardship for disobedience in surah

20, but not in surah 2. Adam's repentance is described in surah 2 and not 20. Take the two versions, and even the third in 7:19-25, and you will find that Adam did repent, suffer hardship and death, and that Satan was his enemy. Knowledge of what happened is increased, and ambiguity clarified.

Biblical examples will clarify what Muslims and some Christians find inconsistent. The act of creation is described in the first two chapters of the book of Genesis. The first chapter says that man was created last of all. The second chapter places his creation before that of animals. Can anyone imagine that men would be so stupid as to record such immediate error? There is no inconsistency. Chapter one shows the majesty of God in creation, and chapter two is centred around man. Chronological order is not employed, as is often the case with the *Bible*. The verses and surahs of the *Qur'an* are not written in their chronological order of descent. If one says, "A man went to London, he took a train," or "A man took a train and went to London," one is free of contradiction. If Genesis 2 is in chronological order, then Adam was created before the garden and placed in it twice. The chapter rather elaborates upon Adam's creation. He was lonely. God had already created the animals and he brought them to him. Adam was not comforted until Eve was created. The account does not mean that God was experimenting to find out what would please Adam. He was emphasizing the need of the sexes, one for the other. This is stressed at the end of the chapter. Adam said: "This is now bone of my bones and flesh or my flesh" (v. 23). Genesis 1 states the fact of the creation; Genesis 2 adds more detail. There is no inconsistency in the descriptions.

The genealogy of Christ in Matthew 1 tells of Joseph the son of Jacob, while Luke 3 calls him son of Heli. The reference is to Joseph, Mary's husband. They aimed to show that Jesus was of Abraham's and David's line, therefore the fulfilment of the prophecies regarding the one who will sit on David's throne.

Genealogies in Christ's day were according to the father and not the mother as is done today for expediency. Jesus was known to his contemporaries as the son of Joseph the carpenter, being Joseph's legal son. Matthew shows that Jesus was the legal heir to David's throne. Luke wrote the genealogy of Mary, daughter of Heli, to show that Jesus was the natural heir to David's throne. Heli had no sons. Joseph, his son-in-law, was regarded by Jewish tradition as being Heli's son in such a case. Luke had to say that Jesus was the son of Joseph, son of Heli, because he could not say, the son of Mary, daughter of Heli. What he did was to continue Heli's genealogy in Joseph, his daughter's husband.

The combined narratives of the thieves on the cross reveal more information than one narrative would. Matthew and Luke said that the thieves cursed Jesus. Luke said that one rebuked the other (Mt.27:44; Mk.15:32; Lk.23:29-43). What happened was that both thieves cursed Jesus, until one saw his patient suffering and repented.

The *Gospel* accounts differ because the inspiration of God's Spirit upon the writers did not affect their personality. It is like reporters covering a train crash. One concentrates upon the injured, another upon the condition of the track and signal boxes, another upon the driver and the speed of travel, and another upon the speed of help arriving. More information is obtained from all accounts than from one. This is why some people read more than one newspaper.

Some *New Testament* writers did not quote exactly from the Old. It is like a man away from his home in London on business. He may say of his return, I am going back to London, or I am going back home. Both statements are accurate. Besides, *New Testament* writers translated into Greek what they read in Hebrew.

Subjects Addressed

The sermon on the mount (Mt.5-7; Lk.6) has been wrongly taken by many as the rule of life for all men. It is not the code of behaviour for civil governments, but for Christian believers. Jesus addressed his disciples (Mt.5:1,2). It is the Christian who should not avenge himself for personal injury. Jesus did not teach that countries should open their borders to invading armies. He said of this matter: "What king, going to war with another king, sits not down first and consults whether he be able with ten thousand to meet him that comes against him with twenty thousand?" (Lk.14:31). The Christian knows that to hate a person is as evil in God's sight as to kill him; to think of adultery is as evil as to commit it.

Computation of Time

Two dates stood for the start of the year in the Jewish calendar: the religious, which fell in March/April, and the secular, which fell in September/October. Part of a year or a day was reckoned for a whole year or day. If a king ruled for three years and twenty days, he would have been regarded as having ruled for four years. Thus one king and his successor would have governed during the same year.

The sign of Jonas has troubled many. Jesus said of himself: "As Jonas was three days and three nights in the whale's belly, so shall the Son of man be three days and three nights in the heart of the earth" (Mt.12:40). From Friday evening, the time of his burial, to Sunday morning, the time of his resurrection, there are one evening, two nights, one day, and part of a day. If Friday and Sunday each counted for a day, as was the custom, then we have three days and three nights. The immigration laws of the United Kingdom provide a good example of this. If a man departs after 12 noon, he is regarded as having stayed the full day in the U.K. If a man arrives on Friday evening, and leaves at 12.05 p.m. on Sunday, he is regarded to have stayed in the country from Friday after midday until midday Monday, that is three days and three nights. There is no error in the statements of Jesus.

The Hebrew Language

The Hebrew language, like the Arabic and other Semitic languages, is based upon root verbs of three consonants without vowels or dots. The *Qur'an* was written in this form. A two-consonant example in English is "bt"— which could be read as bat, beat, boat, bet, bit, or but. Vowels were added in Uthman's time, about the same time that the Masoretes introduced vowels into the Hebrew language. Misreading of the text was possible. Khalifah, with an 'f' and Khaliqah with a 'q', differed by one dot over the letter. One meant "successor," the other "creation."

The other peculiarity of the Hebrew language, which it shares with the Arabic, is the similarity of some of its alphabetical letters. The Dalet (d), and the Raysh (r) provide the simplest example. Letters were used to represent numbers, as seen in the sections of Psalm 119. The Greeks used this method, and we use it today. We write (a), (b), and (c), for (1), (2), and (3). The letters of the alphabet, taken in order, supplied the values of one to ten, the multiples of ten, then 100. Marks or dots were used for thousands. Bet (b), the second letter of the alphabet, stood for two; Bet with a dash above it stood for 2,000. Scribes could mistake the Dalet for a Raysh which stood for 200. Errors could occur in proper names and in numbers. Hadadezer (2Sam.8:3) could easily become Hadarezer (2Sam.10:16). Seven hundred horsemen are said to have been captured by David in 2 Sam. 8:4, and 7,000 in 1 Chr. 18:4. The latter number must be correct, since 20,000 footmen and 1,000 chariots were also taken. A mistake occurred between the final Noon (n) and a dotted Zayin (z).[6] Some numbers were rounded off, others written as multiples—for example 100 would become two 50s.

INTERPRETATION MUST BE INHERENT IN THE TEXT

The *Qur'an* and the *Bible* must be their own interpreters, a vital principle of exegesis. Difficult sections are interpreted in the light of related simpler sections. Where it says in the *Qur'an* that man was created in the best stature (90:4) yet weak (4:28), we must return to the story of his creation and subsequent development.

The Role of Tradition, Mythology and Ritual

The traditions of Islam in the *Hadith*, were said by the Companions of Muhammad and originated in him. The Shi'ites accept the traditions that go back to Ali bin abi Taleb. Traditions increased during the first two Islamic centuries and ceased after the third. Al-Bukhari (194-256 A.H.) distilled just over 7,000 reliable traditions from 600,000.[7] Muhammad bin Idris ash-Shafi'i, of the second Islamic century, noted that traditions should only be accepted where they confirm the *Qur'an*. This is the voice of reason.

Islamic interpretation of the *Qur'an* is fraught with superstition and mythology. When the *Qur'an* says that Adam ate of a tree, the Arabic commentators conjectured about the nature of the tree. They said it was the vine, the fig, the palm, the wheat, the tree of righteousness or, according to some, God knows what it was. Its fruit was sweeter than honey, softer than the cream of cows. Adam was forty years in a state of clay. He was cast out of the garden between 9 A.M. and 10 A.M. He landed in India, or between Makkah and Ta'if, with his hands upon his knees and his head bent forward. Eve landed in Jeddah, the devil not far from Basrah, and the serpent in Asbahan. The devil organized the cats, large and small, led by a vicious dog, to attack Adam. As soon as Adam landed, the devil said to the dog, "This is your enemy, get him!" The angel Gabriel told Adam to caress the dog upon its head. This stilled its viciousness and the animals scattered.[8,9,10]

What does it matter when Adam was thrown out of the garden, or whether he landed in India, Arabia, or Timbuktu? The important point is that Adam the sinner could not remain in paradise. Tales serve the cause of ignorance and divert the minds of the gullible from the real issues. The Jewish rabbis told tales in their interpretation of the *Torah*. Some of these are recorded in the *Qur'an*, such as the story of Abraham when he destroyed his father's idols and escaped the fire (21:51-70). Another is that Solomon knew the language of birds (27:16-21). The Jewish tales have been gathered by Ginzberg in *The Legends Of The Jews*[11] and are found in the *Jewish Encyclopaedia*. The *New Testament* era had its share of apocryphal gospels and epistles. The gospel of Thomas, for instance, claims like the *Qur'an* (3:49; 5:110) that Jesus created a bird out of clay. The day of creation had long gone. Creatures are created through the process of reproduction or procreation. Jesus would not have created life out of nothing.

The *Qur'an* supports tradition. "O believers, obey God and obey the messenger and those in authority over you. If you quarrel over anything refer it to God and the messenger" (4:59). The verse came as a result of a dispute between Khalid ibn el-Waleed and 'Ammar bin Yasir.[12,13]

"Whosoever obeys the messenger obeys God" (4:80) calls men to pay heed to what Muhammad said and did. "Whatsoever the messenger gives you, take and whatsoever he forbids you, leave alone" (59:7) was said of the spoils of war. A precedent was laid that whatever Muhammad ordered and judged was to be regarded as the will of God. Thus the traditions regarding washing, prayer, fasting, marriage, the Haj, and every detail of life, form with the *Qur'an*, the basis for Islamic practice, despite the fact that many of the practices and details are not found in the *Qur'an*.

If one looks at the matter dispassionately, one finds that the doctrines of Islam and its practical foundations are found in the *Qur'an*. The traditions add the ritualistic element to religious duties. The *Qur'an* says pray; the *Hadith* tells you how. The *Qur'an* says, perform the Haj; the *Hadith* tells the details of how it should be done. The *Qur'an* does not give sufficient practical advice for the ritual in religion.

What, then, is the value of ritual or tradition? The children of Israel were bound by temporary ritual until the coming of Christ. The ritual was symbolic of truths that had to be ingrained into them. The laying of the hands of the priest upon the scapegoat signified the laying of the sins of the people on someone else. Such signs pointed to Christ. They were images that helped the people understand, and that kept the remembrance forever before their eyes. Ritual points to the truth. It can never be the truth. It has no value in and of itself. The symbol can never be the reality it represents. The flag is not the nation. This is where people have erred. By thinking that the mechanical observation of ritual had some benefit, they allowed themselves to be blinded by the symbols at the expense of the truth. When you think that you have done a good deed by stoning the devil at the Haj, or that you have finished with the devil, you delude yourself. The stoning is meant to signify that you reject the devil with all your heart. The Lord abhorred the sacrifices of the children of Israel when injustice was rampant. "I will have mercy and not sacrifice" (Hos.6:6). The Roman Catholic Church got bogged down with traditions and ritual, such as the orders of monks and nuns and monastical life, of celibacy, the adoration of Mary, the lighting of candles, prayers for the dead, confession to priests with authority to absolve from sin, of Masses and carrying of crosses and images, of kneeling to images, holy days and holy waters, and sundry other practices. People feel that they have performed their duty towards God if they performed the traditions. God is not satisfied with appearances. He needs hearts that are perfect towards him.

The *Qur'an* says: "This day I have perfected your religion, and I have completed my blessing upon you, and I have approved Islam for your religion" (5:3). It cannot be imagined that this religion is not basically embodied in the *Qur'an*. If the *Qur'an* depends upon extraneous traditions of men for its interpretation, then it is deficient of itself.

THE IMPLICATIONS MUST BE WORKED OUT

Interpretation can be tested by its implications. If, for example, God created Adam with good and evil within him, then God is the source of evil, and is divided in his nature. If the *Qur'an* is eternal because it has always been in the mind of God, then everything is also eternal because it has always been in the mind of God. The implications show the fallacies of the arguments.

COPYIST ERRORS

Certain discrepancies appear in the *Qur'an* and the *Bible*. They were made by scribes who copied the manuscripts. The books as originally given were error-free. Fortunately the errors do not detract from basic doctrines.

Many of the books of the *Bible* were written 2,500 years ago, while the most ancient preceded them by 800 years. Original manuscripts did not survive conquest and pillage. Most Biblical errors are trivial.

The *Qur'an* contains copyist errors. It was gathered from material already written and not from memorized texts.[14] Men heard the *Qur'an* and transcribed it into writing. Mistakes occurred, especially that the *Qur'an* is said to have come down in seven dialects. Add to this the difficulties which the Arabic language shared with the Hebrew, in that it was written without vowels and dots, and the field is open for error. Some errors will be discussed.

"But of them, the firmly rooted (rasikhoon) in knowledge, and the believers (mu'minoon) believing in what has been sent down to you and what was sent down before you, and the performers (muqimeen) of prayers, and those who come with (mu'toon) alms, and the believers (mu'minoon) in God and the last Day, those we shall give them a great wage" (4:162). The word 'muqimeen' is the odd word out, having been used in the objective rather than the subjective form demanded by the sentence. 'Aisha, Muhammad's wife, said that it was a copyist error.[15] As-Suyuti gave six different explanations that attempted to get round the error, without success.[16] 'Aisha added that Muhammad used to recite 'mu'toon' in the same verse, as 'ya'toona ma ato,' meaning those who bring of what they received.

"Surely these two are sorcerers" (20:63). "Surely these two" is written in the *Qur'an* as 'inna hathan,' which is incorrect. The intensifying particle 'inna' demands that the objective form 'hathain' be used, and not 'hathan.' The error is ascribed to the writing of an 'a' or Aleph, instead of the letter 'ya,' designated as 'ai' here.[17]

The writing of numbers is peculiar and complicated in Arabic when words are used. Common nouns are given either a feminine or masculine gender with special rules for the numbers that describe them. For numbers up to two, the feminine form of the number is used with a feminine noun, and the masculine number with a masculine noun. For numbers between three and ten, the position is reversed: the feminine number is used with a masculine noun, and the masculine number with the feminine noun. In numbers added to ten, the ten becomes masculine with a masculine noun and feminine with a feminine noun. Thus in the number twelve, both the two and the ten are masculine with a masculine noun, and feminine with a feminine noun.

A passage in 7:160 uses the feminine form for two and ten with a masculine noun, instead of the masculine form. It says for twelve tribes: 'ithnata 'asharat 'asbatan.' It should have said 'ithnai 'ashar sibtan.' Another peculiarity of the Arabic language is to use the singular form for common nouns with numbers above ten. It says twelve day, and not twelve days. This is why 'sibtan' is correct and 'asbatan' is incorrect. The singular form for fountain is correctly used in the same verse, as are the feminine forms of two and ten with this feminine noun. The singular for fountain is also used in 2:60, with a similar structure of feminine numbers as its use in 7:160. Three, seven, and ten are used correctly in 2:196.

Three incorrect words remain in the *Qur'an*, and give a new meaning to the text. "Do not enter houses other than your houses until you ask leave and salute the people" (24:27). "Ask leave" would be 'ista'thinu' in Arabic. The *Qur'an* says 'ista'nisu,' which means, "become sociable." As-Suyuti quotes those who said it was a scribal error.[18]

"Did not believers know that if God willed he would have guided men all together?" (13:31). The word translated "know" means "to despair" in the *Qur'an*. The same reference says that the scribe was sleepy when he wrote 'yay'as' instead of 'yatabayyan,' which means "to make manifest."

"And your Lord decreed that you shall not serve any but him" (17:23). The word for "decreed" is 'qada' in the *Qur'an*. It means he "settled," "terminated," "concluded," or "closed." The same reference says that the Waw (w) was written with a long tail so that it became stuck with the letter Sad (s as in song), thus giving the impression of the wrong word. The word should have been 'wassa,' that is, he "commended," or "counselled" or "gave charge."

Why should men be afraid of copyists' or scribes' errors in the *Qur'an*? Men are not made infallible when they copy sacred script. Infallibility rests with those who were inspired in the first place. What people heard from Muhammad was the *Qur'an* without error. When they wrote down the verses, errors entered the script due to human fallibility. Correction of the script was made in the days of 'Uthman bin 'Affan, when ibn Ka'ab was in charge of the documents as they were collected.[19] As-Suyuti mentions that the word 'fa-mahhel' in 86:17, meaning "give respite," was originally written on the goat's shoulder as 'fa-'amhel,' meaning "slow down." The teller of the story told how ibn Ka'ab rubbed out the Aleph as he watched. Another word in 2:259 'yatasannah,' for "becoming stale," was originally written without the Ha (h), meaning "to become facilitated or possible." The 'h' was added as the teller watched. The third verse on the goat's shoulder was 30:30: "There is no changing in God's creation." The word 'li-khalq' for creation was originally 'lil-khalq', which is wrong. The second 'l' was rubbed out as the teller watched. Such corrections were right and commendable. There were several versions of the *Qur'an* from which 'Uthman's version was gathered. He burnt all versions except the official one,[20] but returned Hafsa's version to her as he promised. She was Muhammad's wife. Some misinterpret 15:9 which says: "We have sent down the remembrance and we preserve it." The *Qur'an* is still with us today. God did not promise to make scribes infallible.

LIMIT OF HUMAN UNDERSTANDING

One cannot find answers to the problems of religion. Those who want every question answered before they believe never come to faith. Certain matters belong to God alone. The ultimate purpose of the creation is not known. That God wants the friendship and worship of man is a partial answer. God does not need man. What of those who end up in hell? Their misery is too great to imagine. Why did Adam disobey when everything was in his favour? What is the ultimate origin of evil? We must believe what the scriptures say, even though we do not have the ultimate answers.

SUMMARY

The *Qur'an* and the *Bible* were written in the language of men. They are bound by the grammatical and interpretive rules of their languages.

This is particularly so with the Arabic. The *Qur'an* preserved it in its purest form since the seventh century A.D. Knowledge is important for a proper interpretation but monopoly of interpretation is not right. The restriction of interpretation to certain men is the first step in the process of shackling the mind and the masses. This happened in Roman Catholicism when the *Bible* was not to be read or interpreted except by the priests. When a man follows what he is told without thought and consideration of other possibilities, he becomes a slave to his masters. The principle spills over into all aspects of life, creating a nation whose mind is not free and whose sons are not independent.

Knowledge of the context and historical setting is basic to interpretation. Certain verses of the *Qur'an* came to deal with special events, and are not generally applicable. The holy books must be their own interpreters. Verses and passages should be compared, and the ambiguous explained in the light of the clear. Contradiction must be avoided. The implications of any interpretation must always be worked out. Copyist errors must be acknowledged. They explain apparent contradiction in the text, but do not diminish basic doctrine.

References

1. Al-Bukhari, vol.6, pp.207,181,198.
2. Abdul-Hasan Ali bin al-Wahidi, Asbab nuzool el-Qur'an, Jeddah, 1984, pp.32,33.
3. Ibn Hisham, Asseratu-an-nabawiyyah, (Dar ul-Jeel, Beirut), vol.3, pp.14-43.
4. Ibid. pp.200-203.
5. Jalal ud-Deen abd er-Rahman as-Suyuti in Al-Qur'an ul-Kareem, Interpretation and Explanation, by Hasanain Muhammad Makhloof, (Dar ul-Kitab el-Arabi, Beirut). pp.167,168.
6. John W. Haley, Alleged Discrepancies of the Bible, (Baker Book House, Michigan, 1989), p.328.
7. Al-Bukhari, Introduction in vol.1.
8. Al-Fakhr-ed-Deen ar-Razi, Attafseer ul-kabeer, (Dar Ihia' et-Turath el-Arabi, Beirut).
9. Abu Abdullah Muhammad bin Ahmad el-Ansari el-Qurtubi. (Al-jami' le-ahkam el-Qur'an, (Dar Ihia' et-Turath el-Arabi, Beirut).
10. Abu el-Fida' Isma'il bin Katheer al-Qurashi ad-Dimashqi, (Dar Ihia' et-Turath el-Arabi, Beirut).
11. Louis Ginzberg, The Legends of the Jews (The Jewish Publication Society of America, Philadelphia, 1968), vol.1, pp.194-215; vol.5, pp.215-218; vol.4, pp.138,139,142,163; vol. 6, pp.288,289.

12. Al-Wahidi, Ibid. pp.152,153.
13. As-Suyuti, Ibid. pp.112,113.
14. As-Suyuti, al-Itqan fee 'uloom el-Qur'an, ('Alam ul-Kutub, Beirut), vol.1 p.58.
15. Ibid. p.182.
16. Ibid. p.184.
17. Ibid.
18. Ibid. p.185.
19. Ibid. p.183.
20. Al-Bukhari, vol.6, p.226.

Chapter Four
Human Exaggeration

Muslims claim for the *Qur'an* what it does not claim for itself. They close their minds to other possibilities. Such possibilities will be discussed here.

THE QUR'ANIC CHALLENGE

The *Qur'an* is said to have challenged mankind with its eloquence and style. The challenge has not been met. "And if you are in doubt concerning what we have sent down on our servant, then bring a surah like it, and call your witnesses apart from God, if you are truthful, and if you do not, and you will not, then fear the fire whose fuel is men and stones, prepared for unbelievers" (2:23,24; 10:38; 11:13).

The verse is grossly misinterpreted by Muslims. The circumstances of its utterance are not considered, nor the purpose for which it was uttered. Hand in hand with the verse goes the understanding that Muhammad was illiterate (7:157,158). The verse is said to claim a supernatural eloquence and style for the *Qur'an*, thus proving Muhammad to have been the final messenger of God. The matter arises out of an uncertainty in the Muslim's mind. All the major prophets were supported by overt miracles. Muhammad was not. In order to prove that he was a prophet, Muslims devised that the *Qur'an* was his miracle. This verse supports their claim.

Muslims are ready to acknowledge that the *Qur'an* loses a great part of its strength when it is translated into other languages. Translation denudes it of some of its eloquence and weakens some of its ideas. It is the content that matters, and not the verbal dressing. The *Bible* has many passages more eloquent than the *Qur'an*, even when translated. The book of Job has no equivalent, nor the book of Psalms. The eloquence of Isaiah or Habakuk is amazing. Many of those who do not believe the *Bible* enjoy reading it for its literary value, profound depth, and intimate tenderness. But eloquence has never been brought forth as a sign of its divine origin. The *Bible*, like the *Qur'an*, also contains dull and monotonous passages.

Many of Muhammad's hearers were illiterate. Illiteracy is not a proof of an inability to speak profoundly, as pre-Islamic Arabic poetry shows. Tarafah bin al-Abd lived in the last quarter of the fifth century A.D. He produced one of the "hung poems" of Makkah. He spoke ill of the king 'Umar bin Hind, who determined to have him killed, but feared the tongue of another poet, named al-Multamis. The king promised both poets a reward and sent them to his agent in al-Bahrain with letters in their hands. Al-Multamis doubted the king's benevolence. When they arrived in al-Hira in Iraq, al-Multamis found a lad in the street and asked him: "Can you read?" The lad answered in the affirmative. Al-Multamis opened his letter, and the lad read a command to have him killed in al-Baharin. He urged Tarafah to have his letter read, but he refrained. Tarafah was killed, but al-Multamis escaped with his life.[1,2] The story tells us that some of the great Arabian poets were illiterate.

THE MEANING OF THE CHALLENGE

The challenge said, "Bring a surah like unto it." It did not say, a surah with equal eloquence. The Arab spoke of the desert, the horse and camel, of the night and the dawn, the clouds and rain, of the wind upon the sand, and the deserted home of his beloved, of his chivalry, courage and prowess. He degraded his opponent. Then came Muhammad and said: "God is the light of the heavens and the earth" (24:35). "Fear the fire whose fuel is men and stones prepared for unbelievers." "Praise belongs to God who created the heavens and the earth and appointed the shadows and the light" (6:1). The *Qur'an* spoke of God, the creation, angels, the Last Day, the resurrection of the dead, and the final judgment. The Arabs talked of mundane things, and the *Qur'an* spoke of heavenly things. They glorified themselves, and the *Qur'an* made God glorious. They spoke the language of earth, and the *Qur'an* spoke the language of heaven. How could they bring anything like it? Even Musailamah the Liar fabricated verses similar to the Qur'anic style, but he spoke of base and mean things. The *Qur'an*'s challenge should be understood in its historical setting and with reference to those addressed. Any other explanation is futile.

THE QUR'AN AND SCIENCE

Science is another field in which men have strained at the verses of the *Qur'an* and made them lose all meaning. Once again, their aim was to show the miraculous character of the *Qur'an*. It can be said most categorically that neither the *Bible* nor the *Qur'an* contains any scientific fact which could not have been obtained by human observation. The only exception is the story of the creation, which no man witnessed.

Muslims acknowledge that the *Qur'an* is not a scientific textbook but claim that it lays the foundation of all science because it mentions related things. For example, the physics of light is implied because the *Qur'an* mentions the light; of agriculture because it says that grasses and plants grow in the earth; of oceanography, because it mentions that there are seas in the earth, and so on.[3,4]

EXPANSION OF THE UNIVERSE

"And the heaven, we built it with might, and we are extending it" (51:47) is said to prove the expansion of the universe. The word 'lamosi'oon' which is translated "extended," has the meaning of "being able." This is a more appropriate translation because the *Qur'an* does not use the particle "it." The word describes the ability of God in building the heavens. *Lisanul-Arab*, the exhaustive Arabic dictionary, gives it this meaning. Besides this, the *Qur'an* states that the formation of the heavens has been completed. God "lifted up its vault and fashioned it" (79:27-29). He "decorated it and it has no cracks" (50:6). An unfinished work is not decorated. When the Psalmist says that God "stretches out the heavens like a curtain" (Ps. 104:2), he speaks in the present tense. It cannot be surmised that he meant an expanding universe. He was singing of the power of God.

THE EGG-SHAPED EARTH

Most people have seen photographs of the earth taken from many miles above its surface. Has any described it as being egg-shaped? The *Qur'an* has, according to one author.[5] He uses the *Qur'an* to confirm the slight stretching of the earth in its polar axis. "And the earth thereafter he spread it" (79:30). The Arabic word used is 'dahaha.' The word is misinterpreted to mean that he made it like an egg. The *Hadith* interprets the word as meaning that God brought out of the earth its water and pasture.[6] Isaiah said that God "sits upon the circle of the earth" and spreads the heavens "like a tent" (Is.40:22). The earth is pictured as a circle, and the heavens as a vault.

ORIGIN OF THE EARTH FROM THE SUN

"The heavens and the earth were a mass all sewn up, and we unstitched them" (21:30) and "the earth and what threw it off" (91:6) are verses that are said to teach that the earth split from the sun.[7] What they teach is that the universe started as one mass. The contraction of a cooling earth derived from the sun is erroneously seen in 13:41: "Have they not seen that we come to the land diminishing it from its extremities?"[8] Who could observe the contraction of the planet? Men observe the weathering of the land, the incoming of the sea, and the diminishing of the edges and the sides.

ROTATION OF THE SUN AND EARTH AROUND THEIR AXES

"And the sun runs to its fixed abode" (36:37,38). The theory is built upon the misunderstanding of the use of the preposition "to" in the Arabic text. "To" is incorrectly given the meaning of "in."[9] Though the preposition has twenty-two meanings and uses[10] it does not have the meaning of "in." "In" would indicate that the sun runs around its own axis in its resting place. The matter is far fetched. The *Hadith* says that the sun goes under the throne.[11]

"It behoves not the sun to attain to the moon, neither does the day overtake the night, each swimming in a celestial sphere" (36:40). The *Qur'an* and the *Bible* do not tell us that the earth rotates around the sun, which is relatively fixed. Without this knowledge, we cannot assume that the night and day are a result of the rotation of the earth around its axis. We could assume that the sun rotates round the earth. That the night does not overtake the day is misinterpreted to mean that the two are in a race.[12] The argument misses the point. When one horse overtakes another in a race, they are found at one time running side by side. The *Qur'an* says that this does not take place. The night and day do not meet in the acme of their strength.

Another argument does a great injustice to the *Qur'an*. "And on the day the trumpet is blown, terrified were those in the heavens and earth, excepting whom God willed, and all of them came to be humbled. And you see the mountains, and suppose they are fixed, and they pass like clouds" (27:87,88). The argument is that the mountains are mobile with a rotating earth, and not fixed as they appear to be.[13] The author is astounded that commentators ascribe the verses to the resurrection day. He insists that the mountains will be blown up on that day and crumble (20:105; 77:10; 56:5). He then says: "I think contradiction here is quite evident, and the two explanations cannot go in line together for the simple reason that the mountains will not be in existence then." This interpretation is typical of those who do not compare verses with verses adequately, and are willing to close their eyes to what does not suit their ideas. They end up in an absolute muddle. The *Qur'an* certainly refers to the resurrection day: "On that day, we shall set the mountains in motion" (18:47); "and upon that day when heaven spins dizzily and the mountains move in motion, woe shall be on that day unto those that cry lies"; "the day when they shall be pitched in the fire of hell" (52:9-13). "And when the trumpet is blown, and you come, and you shall come in crowds, and the heaven is opened and becomes gates, and the mountains set in motion and become a mirage. Surely hell has become an ambush" (78:91-21). Verse 81:3 says the same thing, while 70:9 says that the mountains will be as tufts of wool. Nothing can be clearer. The day of judgment and resurrection is meant in these verses, when unbelievers will be sent to hell. The mountains will be set in motion also. If the author finds contradiction, then it is not in the interpretation, but in the *Qur'an*. He thus falsifies the *Qur'an*, although I am sure unintentionally, in order to prove a false point. Why should not the mountains be moved from their fixed places and shaken like the wind shakes a tree, and destroyed out of existence upon that day?

INNERVATION OF THE SKIN

A friend came to me to tell of his amazement at the knowledge which the *Qur'an* displays about the innervation of the skin. The skin is rich in pain fibres, therefore the *Qur'an* says of those in the fire, that "whenever their skins are roasted, we shall give them in exchange other skins that they may taste chastisement" (4:56). Who does not know that burning is painful? If you tell the dentist that your tooth hurts you, does it mean that you know how the tooth is innervated? Visceral pain—like the colic of passing a kidney stone—a blow on the bone, the nerve root pain in the arm from a disc lesion in the neck, can be extremely severe. But it is mental agony that drives people to do away with their lives.

EMBRYOLOGY

"Was he not a spermdrop deposited? Then he was a blood clot" (75:37,38). "And of the clot we created a mouthful of tissue and we created of the mouthful bones and we clothed the bones with flesh, thereafter we produced him another creature" (23:13-15). Is this a treatise on embryogenesis or a statement that the child grows in it mother's womb, and that God creates his muscles and bones? The systems develop simultaneously. The muscles do not await the development of the bones. The embryo is attached to the uterus by means of a vascular tissue which forms the placenta. This bloody mass may be described as a blood clot, but it is not the embryo which develops inside a surrounding layer of cells containing fluid.

CONCLUSION

Many so-called scientific facts of the *Qur'an* are a misinterpretation of simple verses. The scientific knowledge contained in the *Bible* and the *Qur'an* could in all cases be obtained through human observation from time immemorial. The account of the creation is a separate issue, and in any case cannot be proved scientifically.

References

1. Abu Abdullah al-Husain bin Ahmad az-Zawzani, Sharh ul-Mu'allaqat us-Sab', (Dar ul-Qalam, Beirut), p.58.
2. Butrus ul-Bustani, Udabaa ul-Arab (Dar Maroon 'Abbood, Beirut, 1979). vol.1, p.117.
3. Afzalur Rahman, Qur'anic Sciences, (The Muslim Schools Trust, London, 1981).
4. Ahmad Mahmud Soliman, Scientific Trends in the *Qur'an*. (Ta-Ha Publishers, London, 1985).
5. Ahmad Mahmud Soliaman, Ibid. p.16.
6. Al-Bukhari, vol.6, p.160.
7. Ahmad Mahmud Soliman, Ibid. pp.20,21.
8. Ibid. p.30.
9. Ibid. pp.19,20.
10. Butrus ul-Bustani, Muheet ul-Muheet, (Maktabat Lubnan, Beirut, 1983).
11. Al-Bukhari, vol.6, p.154.
12. Ahmad Mahmud Soliman, Ibid. p.18.
13. Ibid. pp.16,17.

Chapter Five
The Alleged Sinlessness of the Prophets

Muslims maintain that the prophets were perfect and pure and that God restrained them from great and small sins.[1,2] Some limit the definition of purity to abstinence from the weighty sins. These are, according to the *Hadith*: sharing a god with God, unlawful killing, appropriation of the property of orphans, fleeing from battle before unbelievers, false accusation of believing chaste women, persistence in little sins, false witness, adultery, theft, disobedience to parents, wine drinking, despairing of God's mercy and counting one's own life safe from the wrath of God.[3]

It should be said that the claim of the sinlessness of the prophets is an outright contradiction of the *Qur'an*. That the prophets needed the forgiveness and mercy of God should be sufficient to prove the case. The confusion of the word 'stafa,' meaning "chosen," with the word 'safi,' meaning "pure," may have contributed to the misunderstanding. The *Qur'an* says that God chose the prophets. Did that change their nature? He chose the children of Israel (2:40,47,122), yet they committed felonies. "God chose Adam and Noah and the house of Abraham and the house of Imran above all people" (3:33). He did not only choose Abraham, but the members of his household. Were they all sinless? Abraham was a "true man, a prophet" (19:41). God loved Moses and chose him, though he killed a man (20:38-41). He fulfilled his grace upon Joseph, Abraham, Isaac and other prophets (12:6; 19:58; 6:82-86). Surah 21 details the works of several prophets. It calls Isaac, Jacob and Lot righteous (vv.72,75). They did good works (v.73). This means they were upright, law-abiding men—but not sinless. There is nothing else in the *Qur'an* about the subject. If you choose a pony and care for it, does it grow into a horse incapable of stumbling? We shall discuss the cases of some of the prophets.

NOAH

God told Noah before the flood that none of his family would believe if they had not already believed. When the flood came, Noah asked for his unbelieving son's life to be spared. God was angry with him.[4] It is as if he asked God to lay his justice aside and to break his word. His sin was greater than appears. He felt that he deserved punishment and cried: "If you will not forgive me and have mercy on me, I will be of the losers" (11:36-47).

ABRAHAM

Abraham said, "I crave that he will forgive my sin on the day of judgment" (26:82). Can you believe the following explanation: "We do not know of a sin which Abraham had, but we know that God took him as a friend and shed upon him the qualities of perfection worthy of him." He was chosen, and will be righteous in the next world, and was not an idolater (2:130; 16:120-122). "His request that God should forgive his sin was not a sin in the same meaning that enters the mind, but it was what he felt within himself, a shortcoming of not being lost in God, and a shortcoming in the delivery of his message, due to God's high standing and lofty position."[5] Language has become meaningless. "Forgive me" means I have done no wrong. "Sin" means perfection. The Arabic says: "I am greedy that he will forgive me." His desire for forgiveness was intense. He was an idolater and worshipped heavenly bodies, until God guided him (6:74-83). God was angry with him thrice.[6] This confirms the Biblical record that he lied about his true relationship with Sarah for fear of his life (Gen.12:11-20; chap. 20).

MOSES

Moses killed an Egyptian and blamed the devil: "This is of the work of Satan: he is a manifest enemy." "My Lord, I have wronged myself, therefore forgive me. And he forgave him" (28:15, 16). The incident took place before God called Moses. He was chosen from his infancy and protected by God (20:39-41), yet his sin angered God.[7]

Moses is shown in 18:60-86 to have been impatient. The commentators said that he had a high esteem of himself. He was even proud that God favoured him. God wanted to show him his shortcomings and ignorance.

DAVID

The Qur'anic version is found in 38:21-25. Two brothers asked David to judge between them. One had ninety-nine ewes, yet he took his brother's one ewe from him. "And David thought that we had only tried him; therefore he sought forgiveness from his Lord and he fell down, bowing, and he repented. Accordingly, we forgave him." The case was clear-cut that one brother wronged the other. Why should David feel that he was being tested? Why did he feel guilty and throw himself down on the ground in a crave for forgiveness? We have to look to the *Bible* for the answer. It is found in 2Sam.12:1-14.

David had already committed adultery with Bathsheba, and sent her husband to the front line of the battle, where he was killed. God sent him the prophet Nathan who told him a parable. A rich man had many flocks and herds, and a poor man in the same city had one ewe, beloved of him like a daughter. The rich man took the poor man's ewe and killed it to feed a man who visited him. "And David's anger was greatly kindled against the man; and he said to Nathan: as the Lord lives, the man that had done this thing shall surely die, and he shall restore the lamb fourfold, because he did this thing and because he had no pity. And Nathan said to David, you are the man." He pronounced God's judgment on David and told him that God spared his life; he will not die though he took an oath in God's name that he should die. David saw the fault in someone else, but not in himself. Sin blinds the mind. The kingdom was in turmoil because of sin. His son Absalom rose against him, and David had to flee before him. Psalm 51 details David's anguished cry for forgiveness.

SOLOMON

"When in the evening were presented to him the standing steeds, he said, I have loved the love of good things better than the remembrance of my Lord, until the sun was hidden behind the veil. Return them to me, and he began to strike their shanks and necks. Certainly we tried Solomon and we cast upon his throne a mere body; then he repented. He said, my Lord forgive me, and give me a kingdom such as may not befall anyone after me; surely you are the giver" (38:30-35).

The commentators said that Solomon killed his steeds because they caused him to forget the time of evening prayer. His deed was most heartless and cruel. Like Moses, he blamed someone other than himself for his sin. Some commentators said that he offered the horses in sacrifice to God. This is not true. The horse was not a sacrificial animal.

Why did Solomon repent when according to the *Qur'an*, he saw a body on his throne? Why did he ask for the kingdom to be established? The answer is in the *Bible* (1 Ki.11:1-12). "But Solomon loved many strange women." "He went after Ashtoreth, the godess of the Zidonians, and after Milcom the abomination of the Ammonites, and Solomon did evil in the sight of the Lord." He built "a high place for Chemosh, the abomination of Moab, in the hill that is before Jerusalem, and for Molech"; "and likewise did he for all his strange women, who burnt incense and sacrificed to their gods. And the Lord was angry with Solomon." Solomon committed the great sin of apostasy. God said: "Surely I will rend the kingdom from you, and give it to your servant. Notwithstanding in your days I will not do it, for David your father's sake, but I will rend it of the hand of your son." When Solomon saw the body on the throne, he remembered that the kingdom would go to another, and that his seed would not be established. He asked God to reverse his judgment. The body was not Solomon's as some have said,[8] but was a parable to him. The kingdom was divided after his death into the two kingdoms of Israel and Judah. The *Qur'an* calls Solomon 'awwab' (38:30); this means that he frequently repented. Penitence characterized Solomon's life, because he had much to repent.

MUHAMMAD

Muhammad was reprimanded several times in the *Qur'an*, at times severely, for displeasing God.

The Muslims took prisoners in the battle of Badr in 624 A.D. 'Umar ibn el-Khattab suggested killing them. Others suggested various means of destruction. Muhammad agreed to accept ransom. God said: "It is not for a prophet to have prisoners until he makes a wide slaughter in the land. You desire the chance goods of the present world and God desires the world to come" (8:67). The accusation was of worldly-mindedness and a desire for the accumulation of wealth. Muhammad said, "If punishment descended from heaven, only 'Umar would have escaped."[9]

The Arabs had a custom that a man should not marry his adopted son's daughter who was regarded as his daughter. Muhammad disregarded the custom, but feared to reveal the matter. His adopted son, Zaid bin Harithah, divorced his wife Zainab bint Jahsh, and Muhammad married her.[10] He hid the fact, as Abraham hid the fact that Sarah was his wife. God reprimanded Muhammad for fearing men and annulled the custom (33:37), and said that "Muhammad was not the father of any of your men" (33:40).

When Muhammad sent a military expedition against Tabuk in 631, he permitted some men to stay behind. God rebuked him for his error in judgment and for being taken in by a deception (9:43).

Muhammad was conversing with unbelievers from Quraysh when a blind man entered and interrupted him saying: Teach me what God has taught you. He "frowned and turned away that the blind man came to him;" "but the self-sufficient to him you attend" "and he who comes to you eagerly and fearfully, to him you pay no heed" (80:1-10). Muhammad was not right in his heart. He showed respect of persons.

When Muhammad was a boy, and some say a man, the angel Gabriel took his heart out of his chest and washed it in the well known as Zamzam, then returned it to his chest.[11] Some think that 94:1-3 speak of this, but they do not. How does water cleanse the pollution of the mind? The soul needs more than water to wash its sins away. What guarantee is there that the heart will not become polluted again? We know that it is not sufficient for us to wash once in a lifetime. "Know that there is no god but God, and ask forgiveness for your sins" (47:19), said God to Muhammad. He asked forgiveness for himself and all believers (2:286).

CONCLUSION

All the prophets were sinners because they were born of a sinful seed and had a sinful nature. Jesus Christ was the only exception. This was essential for his task as the redeemer of sinful men.

References

1. Muhammad us-Sadeq Ibrahim Arjoon, Muhammad, Rasool ul-Llah(Dar ul-Qalam, Damascus, 1985), vol.1, p.305.
2. As-Sayyed Sabeq, Al'aq-id ul-Islamiyyat, (Dar ul-Kitab el-Arabi, Beirut, 1985), p.180.
3. Quoted in ibn Katheer's Commentary on the *Qur'an*. vol.1, p.758.
4. Al-Bukhari, vol.6, p.106.
5. As-Sayyed Sabeq, Ibid. p.186.
6. Al-Bukhari, vol.6, p.106.
7. Ibid.
8. Al-Qurtubi's Commentary on the *Qur'an*.

9. Muhammad Rida, Muhammad, Rasool ul-Llah (Dar ul-Kutub el-Islamiyyat Cairo, 1975), p.174.
10. Al-Bukhari vol. 6, p.147.
11. Muhammad Rida, Ibid. p.24.

Chapter Six

The Alleged Corruption of the Bible

A NON-QUR'ANIC CLAIM

Muslims believed for centuries that the Jews tampered with the *Torah*, and the Christians with the *Gospels*. Volumes were written, some with most abusive language and curses against the writers of the *Bible* and the apostles of Christ.[1] Others are not so vehement,[2] but all turn matters upside down. Who of them has seen the original so that he can tell that the copies are inaccurate? The *Qur'an* that you read is only a copy. Does it not carry the same authority as the original? Most criticize the *Bible* today because the descendants of the children of Israel occupied Palestine by so-called divine command. The *Bible* does not teach this highly misunderstood aspect of prophecy. Muslims should not condemn unpalatable doctrines as Israelite.[3,4]

THE QUR'ANIC VIEW OF TAHREEF

Tahreef, in Arabic, is the phonetic changing of the letters of words. Muslims use the word to indicate the changing of the text of the *Bible*. The *Qur'an* repeatedly enforces that the *Bible* is God's word. "A part of them hear the words of God, then they tamper with it after they comprehend it, knowingly" (2:75). "He sent down the Torah and Gospel a guidance for people" (3:3,4), "and gave the Psalms to David" (4:163; 17:55). The *Qur'an* regards the *Torah* in the days of Jesus as the same truth which was given to Moses. God sent "Jesus son of Mary, confirming the Torah between his hands, and we gave him the Gospel, wherein is guidance and light and confirming the Torah between his hands as a guidance and an admonition to the godfearing" (5:46; 3:50). The Torah between his hands, meant the Torah before him, that is the version of his day. If the *Torah* in the days of Jesus was God's word, then it was the same as that sent down upon Moses 1,350 years earlier. The verse also verifies the *Gospel*.

It can be shown from the *Qur'an* that the *Bible* in Muhammad's day was the same authentic *Bible* of years past. "When there has come to them a messenger from God confirming what was with them, a party of them that were given the Book reject the Book of God behind their backs as though they knew not" (2:101). The Book intended was the Jewish book and not the *Qur'an*, according to ar-Razi's and al-Qurtubi's commentaries. Apart from it being called the *Book of God,* and that Muhammad came to confirm it, we must recognize that what is involved is more than the *Torah*. The *Qur'an* says, confirming "what was with them." The book that was with the Jews in Muhammad's time was the Hebrew *Bible*, that is the whole of the *Old Testament*. The Qur'anic verse that follows, that is 2:102, proves the point. It tells of the Jewish misunderstanding of Solomon's faith. Solomon lived 400 years after Moses, and is mentioned in the books of Kings and Chronicles. "You have been given the Book, believe in what we have sent down, confirming the truth of what is with you" (4:47; 5:48). "And when God took the covenant of the prophets regarding what I (God) have given you of the Book and wisdom, then came a messenger confirming what was with you, so that you believe in him and support him" (3:81).

Nothing can be clearer than this. The *Torah*, the writings of the prophets, and the whole of the Hebrew *Bible*, which the Jews had in Muhammad's day, were given by God. The Jews were expected, as a result, to accept Muhammad's message. If Jesus and Muhammad confirmed the Jewish *Bible*, then it did not change from the time of Moses. Extant manuscripts and the Dead Sea Scrolls have shown that the *Bible* has kept its integrity in the past 1,000 years. Who are you, then, to falsify the *Qur'an* you believe in? If the *Bible* had been corrupted, then Muhammad would have destroyed his own message by seeking its confirmation from a corrupt *Bible*.

A CORRUPTION OF SPEECH

"A part of them hear the word of God, then they tamper with it" (2:75). The word "then" indicates that the tampering came after the hearing. It means that the Jews heard God's words in the *Bible*, then deliberately changed their form and meaning, in order to deny Muhammad's continuity with the prophets (2:41,42,91,101,121). The accusation is of a misrepresentation of what the *Bible* said, not of its written text. The tahreef was therefore verbal or interpretive. The *Bible* said one thing, and they said that it said another thing: "A party of them twist their tongue with the Book so that you regard it of the Book, but it is not of the Book" (3:78). They lied in what they said the *Bible* said. They acted likewise: "Do you believe in part of the Book and disbelieve in part"? (2:85). They disobeyed the teaching of the *Bible* by taking prisoners of their own people. The *Bible* said one thing and they did another.

You may ask, what about 2:79? "Woe unto them who write the book with their hands and say it is from God." According to Muslim tradition,[5,6,7,8] the Jews changed the description of Muhammad in the *Torah*. The tradition is false. The *Bible* does not deal with such trivialities. If a man is called of God, who cares about his height and the colour of his hair and eyes? The word "write" is in the present continuous tense. It means that the Jews wrote in Muhammad's day what they regarded as God's words. It was not the copying of the *Bible*, but of something new. The *Bible* had been completed centuries before Muhammad. What did the Jews write? The answer is that they wrote the traditions of the *Midrash*. The *Midrash* is an exposition of Biblical verses. The other Jewish books were the *Talmud* and the *Mishnah*. The *Mishnah* is a collection of writings dealing with matters of social and religious behaviour. The *Talmud* is an exposition of the *Mishnah*. The books were written by Jewish rabbis, and have no divine authority. They were both complete before Islam. The *Midrash* remained open until the thirteenth century A.D.[9] The meaning of 2:79 becomes a reprimand for writing the *Midrash* and saying it was from God.

Verbal corruption is also mentioned in verses like 4:46 and 5:13. "Of those who become Jews are some who pervert words from their places," that is take them out of their context in the written script, in order to give them a new meaning. Others "conceal from the content of the Book" (5:15), in order to deny the mention of Muhammad in the *Book*. The *Hadith* confirms this interpretation.[10] The people of the *Book* should have listened to their books. (5:66). "You do not stand on anything until you perform the Torah and the Gospel and what was sent down to you from your Lord" (5:68). "Why do you confound the truth with vanity and conceal the truth, and that wittingly?" (3:71). "They are silent about the truth" (2:146). The Qur'anic view of the corruption of the *Bible* is clearly that of verbal misrepresentation and of hiding the truth which pointed to Muhammad.

SUMMARY

It is said that Muhammad could not read. The Arabic *Bible* was not in existence then. The Christians of Arabia could not read their *Bible*. Only the Jews possessed their manuscripts. These were written in Hebrew.[11] Muhammad and the Arabs had no access to them, despite claims to the contrary. This is why the *Qur'an* said; "Bring the Torah now, and recite it if you are truthful" (3:93). It did not say, "bring it and let us look at it, but 'recite it,'" that is, you alone could read it. How could the Jews disprove Muhammad's claim that the *Bible*'s message differed from his? No one else could read the evidence. The matter is not so in our day. The *Bible* is available in most languages of the world. It is easy to see that its central message is salvation by the blood of Christ. The *Qur'an* denies that he died. It nullifies the very basis of the *Bible*'s message. Perhaps Muslims have seen that the Biblical message is completely different from the Qur'anic message regarding the way back to God, and invented the false theory that the *Bible* has been corrupted. Unfortunately they find themselves disputing with the *Qur'an* in this matter. It regards the *Bible* as God's words, and never says that its text has been tampered with. The best example of tahreef I can give is the Islamic method of misinterpreting the verses of the *Qur'an* which we discussed, and concluding from them that the Biblical text had been tampered with.

References

1. Abu Muhammad bin Ahmad, known as ibn Hazm adh-Dhahiri, Al-fasl fee Imilal wal-ihawa' wan-nihal, (Dar ul-Jeel, Beirut, 1985), vol.1 & 2, throughout.
2. Laila Hasan Sa'ad ed-Deen, Surah 62:5, p.15
3. 'Aisha Abd ur-Rahman, Al-Qur'an wa-qadaya el-Insan, (Dar ul-'Ilm lil-Malayeen, Beirut, 1982), p.33
4. Fathi Radwan, Al-Islam wal-Muslimoon, (Dar ush-Sharq, Cairo, 1982), p.450.
5. Al-Qurtubi's Commentary on the Qur'an.
6. Ar-Razi's Commentary on the Qur'an.
7. As-Suyuti in Makhloof's version of the Qur'an, p.10.
8. Al-Wahidi, p.24.
9. Robert M. Zeltzer, Jewish People, Jewish Thought, (Macmillan Publishing Co. Inc., New York, 1980), p.269.
10. Al-Bukhari, vol.6, p.51.
11. Ibid. p.25.

Chapter Seven

Muhammad and Biblical Prophecy

THE SUFFICIENCY OF CHRIST

The *Qur'an* says that the *Bible* prophesied of Muhammad's advent as the messenger of God. The *Hadith* confirms this.

The *Bible* is mainly concerned with God's redemption in Christ. It was promised from the beginning of time and finally accomplished. Christ is the end of God's revelation by definition, the "author and finisher of our faith" (Heb.12:2). The *Bible* would have destroyed its own message had it prophesied of another to come after him. Jesus said of himself: "I am Alpha and Omega, the beginning and the end, says the Lord, who is and who was and who is to come, the Almighty" (Rev.1:8; 21:6). The opening verses of the epistle to the Hebrews summarize the matter succinctly: "God, who at sundry times and in divers manners spoke in time past unto the fathers by the prophets, has in these last days spoken unto us by his Son;" "who when he had by himself purged our sins, sat down on the right hand of the Majesty on high" (Heb.1:1-3).

Jesus told a parable where the master sent his servants to claim his possession. They were ill treated, so he finally sent his son. After the son was killed the master came with vengeance against them (Mt.21:33-44; Mk.12:1-11). No other messengers were sent. The issue is not whether the *Bible* prophesied of Muhammad or not. It is whether Christ and his work are of vital importance to the human race in God's plan or not. If Christ was not the last word, then the *Bible* and Christianity are redundant. A total rejection of the Christian faith is imperative if Christ is not sufficient. This is the only reason which drives me to discuss the alleged Biblical prophecies regarding Muhammad.

THE QUR'ANIC VERSES

"Jesus, son of Mary, said, children of Israel, I am indeed the messenger of God to you confirming the Torah that is before me, and giving good tidings of a messenger who shall come after me, whose name shall be Ahmad" (61:6). "Those who follow the messenger, the illiterate prophet whom they find written down with them in the Torah and the Gospel" (7:157). Muhammad is "the seal of the prophets" (33:40).

THE BIBLICAL VERSES

Deuteronomy 18:15

Moses said to the children of Israel: "The Lord our God will raise up unto you a prophet from the midst of you, of your brethren, like unto me."

The Muslim's argument is simple: The Arabs are the brothers of the Jews. Jesus was a Jew, Muhammad was an Arab, so the prophecy concerns Muhammad.[1] The fallacy of this argument is evident. First, the promised prophet was coming to the Jews, as shown by the words "unto you." Notice that 61:6, which speaks of Ahmad, says clearly Jesus was sent to the Jews, and Muhammad to the Arabs. Second, the *Torah* says, "from the midst of you" that is from the midst of the Jews. The Jews of Madinah were not representative of world Jewry. The Jews of ancient Israel were. The prophet was to rise from Israel and not Arabia. Third, he was to be of their brethren, that is, of the children of Israel. He was not to be of the nations in their midst, not an Egyptian, Edomite, Moabite, Hittite, Syrian, or Jebusite.

A cardinal rule of interpretation is to compare verses with verses. The *Bible* must be allowed to explain what it means by "of your brethren." The word is used to indicate filial brothers or distant relatives. Moses used it for the intertribal relationships of the children of Israel. When the children of Reuben and of Gad asked to settle on the near side of Jordan, Moses answered: "Shall your brethren go to war and shall you sit here" (Num.32:6). The children of Israel are again called the brethren of Reuben and of Gad (Deut. 3:16-18). Joshua commended them for not leaving their brethren in their war (Josh.22:3-8). Similarly, Levi was not given an "inheritance with his brethren" (Deut.10:9). Thus the members of one tribe were the brethren of the other tribes.

Before Moses promised them the prophet in Deut.18:15, he spoke to them that they might desire a king in the future (Deut.17:15). "You shall in any case set him a king over you whom the Lord shall choose: one from among your brethren shall you set a king over you: you may not set a stranger over you, who is not your brother." God chose Saul of the tribe of Benjamin to be their first king, and after him David, of Judah. Can you imagine that Moses was telling them that their king must be an Arab? Peter, in Acts 3:22-26, and Stephen, in Acts 7:37,38, correctly interpreted Deut.18:15 to refer to Jesus. He was the one through whom all the families of the earth will be blessed, that the promise given to Abraham, Isaac and Jacob be fulfilled.

Deuteronomy 33:2

"The Lord came from Sinai and rose up from Seir unto them; he shone forth from mount Paran and he came forth with ten thousands of saints: from his right hand went a fiery law for them."

Muhammad Rida said that in this last directive of Moses, God shall shine through Jesus from the mountains of Seir in Palestine, and then through Muhammad from the mountains of Paran, which are synonymous with Makkah. The thousands of saints were the companions of Muhammad. The fire in his right hand was the Islamic law which burnt those who attributed a partner with God.[2] As-Sayyed Sabeq said that the rising from Seir refers to the conquest of Seir by David, that Paran was the ancient name for al-Hijaz, where Muhammad appeared and entered Makkah with ten thousand supporters.[3]

The first thing to be said of such interpretations is that Moses spoke in the past tense. He did not prophesy, but related to the people their experience in the desert. The second point is that God came and rose and shone "for them," or on behalf of the same people. He did not come from Sinai for one people and shine forth for another.

Sinai, Seir and Paran were places of significance in the journey of the children of Israel from Egypt to Canaan. It was on Mount Sinai, in the southern part of the Sinai Peninsula, where the Lord gave the law to Moses. Seir is Edom, the land of Esau, Jacob's brother (Gen.32:3; 36:8; Deut.2:4). Edom extended to Elat by the Red Sea (1Ki.9:26).

The king of Edom refused to let the people pass through his land (Num.20:14-22). The Lord forbade the people to attack Edom because of Jacob's relationship to his brother Esau (Deut.2:5; Josh.24:4; 2Chr.20:10). Seir was therefore the last obstacle to their journey north. They had to go around the mountain by going through its eastern border from the south. The Lord carried them through. He rose up from Seir for them. This was the language of the prophets, as Deborah said in Judges 5:4,5: "Lord, when you went out of Seir, when you marched out of the field of Edom, the earth trembled, and the heavens dropped, the clouds also dropped water, the mountains melted before the Lord, even as Sinai from before the God of Israel."

Paran is not Makkah. The Gulf of Aqaba separates Sinai from Arabia. Their aim was Canaan northwards, and not Arabia southwards. They entered the wilderness of Paran when they left the Sinai desert (Num.10:12). Paran was extensive. It included the wilderness of Zin in the northeast. Kadesh was a notable centre for this area. It lay at the outermost part of Edom (Num.20:1,16; 13:26; 27:14). Ain Qedis retains its name, although Kadesh was probably where the greater spring of Ain Qudeirat is situated. Moses sent men to spy the land of Canaan from Kadesh (Num.13:17,26), and others to the king of Edom. This means that they were near their destination, and not far away in Makkah.

Abraham lived in the south country, between Kadesh and Shur (Gen.20:1). The roads went out from Kadesh westwards by way of Shur to Egypt, northwards to Canaan, eastwards to Edom, and southwards to Sinai. Hagar was an Egyptian and, when she was asked to leave Abraham's house, she took Ishmael towards her homeland. It was in the wilderness of Paran that the angel of the Lord met her, and Ishmael dwelt in Paran (Gen.21:14-21). Finally, when David escaped from Saul he went to the wilderness of Paran (1Sam.25:1). Paran extended to the south of Palestine, and has several mountains. Its name persists in Sinai in the names of Wadi Feeran and Feeran oasis. Central Sinai is called at-Teeh, that is the place of wandering. The Lord was a shining light to the people. The cloud led them by day, and the pillar of fire by night. The giving of the Law at Sinai was accompanied by fire and thunderings, witnessed by thousands of people (Ex.24:17).

Isaiah 41:2-4

"Who raised the righteous man from the East, called him to his foot, gave the nations before him and made him rule over kings? He gave them as the dust to his sword and as driven stubble to his bow. He pursued them and passed safely; even by the way that he had not gone with his feet. Who has wrought and done it, calling the generations from the beginning? I the Lord, the first, and with the last; I am he."

It is claimed that Muhammad was the man from the East, the bearer of the sword and the bow, for Jesus did not fight.[4] Neither Muhammad nor Jesus is meant, but King Cyrus of Persia. After the prophecies of woe and destruction against the nations, and against Israel for their sin, and after the Babylonian captivity and the fall of Babylon, Isaiah spoke of the one who would tread down nations. They would tremble before him, "but you Israel are my servant, Jacob whom I have chosen, the seed of Abraham my friend;" "fear not" (Is.41:8,10). The great warrior was to be used by God to return the captivity of his people. The Lord speaks in similar terms later: "Thus says the Lord to his anointed, to Cyrus, whose right hand I have held to subdue the nations before him; and I will loosen the loins of kings" (Is.45:1). The nations "shall fall down to you, they shall make supplication to you," "but Israel shall be saved in the Lord" (Is.45:14,17). Cyrus issued the edict of the return of the captives to the land of Israel and the rebuilding of the temple.

The Paraclete (John 14:16,17,26; 15:26; 16:7-14)

"And I will pray to the Father, and he shall send you another Counsellor (Paraclete), that he may be with you for ever; even the Spirit of truth" (Jn.14:16). The word Paraclete is the cause of the misunderstanding. It has been translated to mean "the praised one," that is, Muhammad.[5] The meaning is incorrect. The word is also used in 1Jn.2:1. It has the meaning of one called to the side, or one who stands by another as his helper.[67] It means an advocate, or one who speaks on behalf of another.

Jesus was leaving his disciples as the time of his crucifixion drew near. He was not to be with them as before, walking in the streets and preaching and teaching. He was going to physically leave them. He promised that he would be with them by his Spirit. He said that he would send another counsellor. The word "another" signifies that he was the first counsellor. "When he, the Spirit of truth is come, he will guide you into all truth . . . and he shall glorify me" (Jn.16:13,14). The Spirit was to be their helper and guide, even as Jesus was when he was with them. He would not be visible, but they would know him and feel his power, for he "shall be in you" (Jn.14:17). Jesus spoke to comfort his disciples. He was not prophesying an event 600 years later. The Spirit was to be sent to them very soon. He told them, just before his ascension, to wait in Jerusalem "for the promise of the Father which, he said, you heard from me," and "you shall receive power after the Holy Spirit is come upon you, and you shall be witnesses to me both in Jerusalem and in all Judea and in Samaria and unto the uttermost part of the earth" (Acts 1:4,8). The Holy Spirit came down upon them, as described in Acts, Chapter 2. The fearful disciples became as fearless lions; they cared not for their lives, but preached Christ crucified and raised. The Church was empowered on that day.

Muhammad Rida asks: If the paraclete does not refer to Muhammad, to whom does it refer? Who came after Jesus to reprove the world of its sin and who is the Spirit of truth who does not speak of himself? Is it not Muhammad?[8] It makes one wonder how well he read the relevant passages in the *Bible*, for they are self-explanatory.

Revelation 19:11-17

"And I saw the heavens opened, and behold a white horse, and he that sat upon it was called Faithful and True, and in righteousness he does judge and make war. His eyes were a flame of fire, and on his head were many crowns; and he had a name written which no man knew, but he himself. And he was clothed with a vesture dipped in blood: and his name is called the Word of God. And the armies which were in heaven followed upon white horses, clothed in fine linen, white and clean. And out of his mouth goes a sharp sword, that with it he should smite the nations: and he shall rule them with a rod of iron: and he treads the winepress of the fierceness of the wrath of Almighty God. And he has on his vesture and on his thigh a name written, KING OF KINGS AND LORD OF LORDS. And I saw an angel standing in the sun; and he cried with a loud voice saying to all the fowls that fly in the midst of heaven, come and gather yourselves together unto the supper of the great God."

Muhammad Rida says: There is no doubt that Muhammad is meant. He used to be called the Faithful, the Truthful. "Out of his mouth goes a sharp sword" refers to the *Qur'an*. Muhammad trod the winepress, meaning that the wine is absolutely forbidden. But Jesus changed water to wine in a wedding in Cana, and said that the wine is his blood.[9] Such, then, is the argument.

The conclusion that Muhammad is intended is beyond comprehension. The person is named the Word of God, a clear reference to Jesus (4:171; Jn.1:1,14). God is the King of Kings and Lord of Lords. He sits on the throne (21:22; 23:86; 27:26). Jesus identified himself with God. His vesture is dipped in blood, because he is the slain lamb who redeemed men by his blood (Rev.5:6,9). He is described with eyes as a flame of fire, and out of his mouth went a sharp two-edged sword (Rev.1:14,16).

The book of Revelation was meant to comfort a persecuted Church in the first century, and to tell them that Christ would defeat Satan and all his enemies. Our verses depict a triumphant Christ, not the humiliated Christ who once stretched his hands out to his crucifiers. He shall judge the world. The kings of the earth, the great, the mighty, the rich, the slaves, the free, shall hide themselves in the dens and rocks and say "fall on us, and hide us from the face of him that sits on the throne and from the wrath of the Lamb: for the great day of his wrath is come, and who shall be able to stand" (Rev.6:15-17).

Grapes were crushed with the feet in order to extract their juice for fermentation. "Treading the winepress of the fierceness of the wrath of God" means the treading and crushing of his enemies like grapes in the winepress.

SUMMARY

The *Bible* never prophesied of Muhammad. Its message is based upon the salvation which God provided through redemption in Jesus Christ. He was that great prophet who was to come of the tribe of Judah, and not of Quraysh. He led the children of Israel as the angel of the Lord through the Sinai desert, into the wilderness of Paran, and round mount Seir in Edom. He sent the Holy Spirit upon the disciples, and he promised to return to judge the world. Did Jesus send Muhammad? One thing comes out of the claim that Muhammad was the paraclete, and that is the acknowledgment by Muslims of the personality of the paraclete. Truly the Holy Spirit is the third person in the blessed Holy Trinity. Finally, Isaiah 41 speaks of King Cyrus and none other.

References

1. Muhammad us-Sadeq Ibrahim Arjoon, Muhammad, Rasool ul-Llah, (Dar ul-Qalam, Damascus, 1985), vol.1, p.24.
2. Muhammad Rida, Muhammad Rasool ul-Llah, (Dar ul-Maktabat el-Islamiyyat, Beirut, 1975), pp.46,47.
3. As-Sayyed Sabeq, Al'aqa-id ul-Islamiyyat, (dar ul-Kitab el Arabi, Beirut, 1985), p.205.
4. Muhammad Rida, Ibid. p.47
5. Ibid. pp.45,46.
6. James Hastings, Dictionary of the Bible, (T&T Clark, Edinburgh, 1963).
7. John L. McKenzie, Dictionary of the Bible, (Collier Books, New York, 1965).
8. Muhammad Rida, Ibid. p.46.
9. Ibid. p.48.

Chapter Eight
The Canon of the Bible

Muslims have one holy book. They find it hard to envisage how the gathered writings of a multitude of men constitute God's word. Yet the unity of the *Bible* is amazing, considering that it was written over 1,500 years by men of varied walks in life—kings, shepherds, scribes, priests, prophets, fishermen and one physician.

The word "canon" originates from a Babylonian word for "reed", or a fixed rule or measuring rod. The canon of the *Bible* refers to the books which compose it. It is regarded as the standard of God. Why were certain books included and not others? Why were the apocryphal books rejected? The answer lies in that the books were recognized as possessing an authority which came from God.

It should not be thought that the books were chosen at random. Their material had to be known by the people and acknowledged as having divine authority. The authority rested with the prophets who preached what the books contained. The authority of Moses, David, Solomon and the prophets of Israel was acknowledged in the same way that Muhammad's authority was acknowledged, and that of Musailamah the Liar rejected. One has to read the apocryphal books to realize that they are far removed from the genuine Biblical books.

THE OLD TESTAMENT

Canonicity depended upon internal and external evidences, the internal being the more important. The Qur'anic testimony for the truth of the *Bible* is discussed when the alleged corruption of the Bible was considered. It will not be discussed further.

The children of Israel accepted the *Torah* as being of God. The commandments were given in their hearing and presence. After the death of Moses God asked Joshua to do according to the law which Moses commanded (Josh.1:7,8). The same instruction was given to David (1Ki.2:3). When Joash, king of Judah, put to death the men who killed his father, "the children of the murderers he slew not, according to that which was written in the book of the law of Moses" (2Ki.14:6). The commandment said: "The fathers shall not be put to death for the children, neither shall the children be put to death for the fathers: every man shall be put to death for his own sake" (Deut.24:16). After the return of the exiles, the temple was rebuilt and dedicated. The arrangement of the priests was according to that prescribed in the "book of Moses" (Ezr.6:18), and the law was read to the people. The book of Malachi, which dates to 420 B.C., carries the injunction that the law of Moses should be obeyed (Mal.4:4). The authority of the *Torah* thus depended upon the God-given authority of Moses.

The authority of the prophets of Israel confirmed the authority of their books. "And all Israel from Dan even to Beer-sheba knew that Samuel was established to be a prophet of the Lord" (1Sam.3:20). His words carried authority to king and beggar alike.

One sign of the prophet's calling was that his words came to pass. "Now in the first year of Cyrus King of Persia, that the word of the Lord spoken by the mouth of Jeremiah might be accomplished, the Lord stirred up the spirit of Cyrus king of Persia" (2Chr.36:22; Ezr.1:1,2). This was in contrast with the case of the false prophets who cried "peace, peace, when there is no peace" (Jer.6:14; 8:11). Jonah's prophecy was confirmed in that he ran away from God, and God would not let him go. His message turned Nineveh's heart towards God and saved it from destruction. Amos said: "I was no prophet, neither was I a prophet's son, but I was an herdman and a gatherer of sycomore fruit: and the Lord took me as I followed the flock and the Lord said unto me, go prophesy unto my people Israel" (Amos 7:14,15). The words of most of the prophets started with, "the word of the Lord which came to," or "the burden of the Lord," or they proceeded to say, "thus says the Lord." They spoke with the authority of God, and the people knew it. The book of Esther does not even mention God. Its importance is in that it tells how God saved his people from extermination, for of them was to come Christ the Saviour.

The important external evidence for the canonicity of the *Old Testament* is that of Christ and his apostles. Jesus explained the prophecies concerning himself from the Law, the Prophets and the Psalms (Lk.24:44). These were the three divisions of the books of the Hebrew *Bible*. He quoted the scriptures frequently, and referred to the passages which would embarrass many people, such as the story of Adam and Eve (Mt.19:3-9; Mk.10:2-9), of Jonah in the fish's belly (Mt.12:39-42; Lk.11:29-32), of Sodom and Gomorrah, and of the flood in the days of Noah. He spoke of many historical and legal matters. His mouth was full of the scriptures. He used them in his arguments with the Jews, and in answering the devil during the days of his temptation in the wilderness (Mt.4; Lk.4).

The apostles of Christ did as he did. The letters to the Galatians and Hebrews are almost exposition of *Old Testament* doctrines. The Apocrypha, which is a collection of books written between 300 B.C. and 100 A.D. and which deals with Jewish history, was never mentioned or quoted from by Jesus or his apostles. The books do not speak in God's name. They were rejected from entering the canon of scripture by the Jewish scholars at Jamnia, near Joppa, in A.D. 90. The introduction to Ecclesiasticus, an apocryphal book written in 200 B.C. and prefaced by the grandson of the author in 130 B.C., regards the books of the *Old Testament* as the Law, the prophets, and the Hymns or Psalms. Josephus (37-100 A.D.) accepted the canon of the *Old Testament* only. The last two verses of Malachi, the last prophet of the *Old Testament*, suggest that the next prophet will be John, who will come in the spirit of Elijah, as the herald of Christ. This took place (Mt.11:14). The Roman Catholic Church erroneously accepted the Apocrypha in 1546.

The Dead Sea Scrolls provide further evidence that only the books of the *Old Testament* were regarded as canonical. They show that the *Torah* has not materially changed between the first century B.C. and today.

THE NEW TESTAMENT

The church, or the household of God, was "built upon the foundation of the apostles and prophets, Jesus Christ himself being the chief cornerstone" (Eph.2:20). The *New Testament* derives its authority from the approval and authority of the apostles. The apostles had to see the risen Christ. Paul was the last apostle. He took his place with the others as if at the eleventh hour (1Cor.9:1). He saw Christ in reality and not in a vision on the Damascus road (Acts 9:1-11). Christ taught him the gospel after that (Gal.1:11-24). Luke was his companion in his work for Christ (Col.4:14; 2Tim.4:11; Phm.24). He told the events "even as they delivered them to us, who from the beginning were eyewitnesses and ministers of the word" (Lk.1:2). Mark was Peter's companion (1Pet.5:13). The epistle to the Hebrews has no named author, but has the mark of God in its teaching. Its author was known to the church to whom it was written. The other writers of the *New Testament* were eyewitnesses of Christ's majesty (2Pet.1:16). John said that they heard and looked upon and their hands handled the Word of Life, and bore witness that he was with them (1Jn.1,2). The *Gospels* are eyewitness accounts by those who were with Christ, and two of their companions. The Epistles were written by the same eyewitnesses, and Christ revealed the gospel to Paul. He did not learn it from the other apostles, who were amazed that he preached the same message (Gal.1:23). All the books of the *New Testament* were written in the first century, when many were still alive to verify the facts.

Apocryphal gospels and epistles were written, but never admitted to the canon for lack of apostolic authority. The gospel of Thomas, for instance, describes Jesus as a malevolent and vicious child.

THE GOSPEL OF BARNABAS

The book was discovered in the seventeenth Christian century. It could not be affirmed by the early Christian Church. It could not therefore rest upon apostolic authority, and can never enter the canon of the *Bible*. The matter should be closed here. But Muslims would have us believe that it is the only authentic account of the gospel of Christ. They would shudder if someone were to ask them to accept Sahih ul-Bukhari, or the Qur'an of Musailamah as the authentic version of the *Qur'an*. Yet this is what they do with the gospel of Barnabas.

I first came across this book when it was quoted in Ahmad Adel Kamal's book, *The Road to Damascus: The Conquest of Syria*.[1] He treated it as if it was of the canon of the Bible. I was later able to find an Arabic copy of a translation of an English version, translated by Dr. Khalil Sa'adeh in 1908.[2]

The Italian version was discovered in the seventeenth century, and was thought to have been copied at the end of the sixteenth century from an unknown source. Dr. Sa'adeh discussed the book in his excellent and scholarly preface. He concluded that it was written in the fourteenth century by a Jew who adopted Islam and who lived in Spain. The book was not known by the Muslim scholars and commentators of the *Qur'an* in the first centuries. They differed in their views as to who died in place of Jesus, while Barnabas categorically says it was Judas Iscariot (Barn.215-217).

Jesus is said to have seen Muhammad (Barn.44:30,31), making

Muhammad pre-existent. The author thought that Nazareth was by Lake Tiberias (Barn.20:1), that Jesus was born when Pilate was governor (Barn.3:2), and that Christ was from Ishmael's seed (Barn.142:17). He attributed Ezekiel's words in 18:32 and 33:11 to Joel (Barn.165:1) and mistook Darius for Cyrus when he referred to Daniel (Barn.50:36). There are numerous other mistakes.

The author went out of his way to praise Muhammad, calling him the messenger of God, in the Islamic way. He denied the crucifixion of Jesus and spoke of the garden, a term never used for heaven in the *New Testament*. He stressed the necessity of circumcision: Jesus said, "I tell you the truth, the dog is preferred to an uncircumcised man" (Barn.22:2). He frequently introduced the words of Jesus by the words, "by the life of God," whereas Jesus forbade the vain and vile use of God's name (Mt.5:34-37). He thought that the Pharisees existed at the time of Elijah. Their movement actually started 400 years later, and branched into a separate body 300 years after that. The philosophical concept of the four elements of matter, fire, water, air and earth is accepted in the book. In fact, the book is a jumble of Islamic and Jewish ideas with errors arising here and there, and with a view to demolish the Christian gospel. It also contradicts the *Qur'an*. Mary is said to have given birth painlessly (Barn.3:10), whereas the *Qur'an* says she travailed and wished she had died (19:22,23). It advocates that a man be content with one wife (Barn.115:18). In short, it is a counterfeit book.

SUMMARY

The Bible tells the history of revelation as it was enacted in time. The authority of each book is found within its pages. The Spirit of God has unified its message, because he is the real author. The immediate derivation of the authority of the books was of the prophets, for the *Old Testament*, and the apostles of Christ for the *New Testament*. The *New Testament* supports the Old, and Jesus frequently quoted the Jewish Bible. The *Old Testament* is fulfilled in the new. The apocryphal books of both eras have no place in the canon of scripture. The so-called gospel of Barnabas is counterfeit, its aim was to deceive. One has to compare it with any of the *Gospels* of the *New Testament* to see the marked difference between the word of man and the word of God.

References

1. Dar un-Nafa-is, (Beirut, 1980), p.139.
2. Published by Muhammad Ali Sabeeh & Sons, (Cairo), Introduction.

Chapter Nine

The Divine Trinity

A great misunderstanding must first be cleared. The *Bible*, like the *Qur'an*, stresses the unity of God. But the *Bible*, contains a revelation that concerns the being of God, which the *Qur'an* does not. The *Qur'an* stresses that God is One, but <u>does not speak of the mode of his exist</u>ence. This mode is the Biblical revelation that the one God exists in the three persons of his being. This cannot be known without divine revelation.

A large number of Muslims think that the doctrine developed in the third and fourth Christian centuries. What happened then was the definition of the doctrine to a church that had gone largely heretical. Denials were made of the divinity of Christ, or of his humanity. The councils of bishops met to resolve the disputes within the church, and issued statements or creeds in an effort to counteract the heresies that arose.

The bare and solitary Oneness of God is easier to fathom than the nature of man himself. Man is body and spirit. His spirit lives after he is dead. It can understand, feel and suffer. If God is a rigid unity, then he is less than his creature.

DEFINITION

The doctrine of the Trinity is that, while God is One, with no partner in his being or kingdom, he is at the same time three persons in indivisible unity, of one substance, eternity, power, equality, and all the divine attributes. The Trinity is a <u>Triunity.</u> This means that there was no time when the Son and the Spirit were non-existent. The One and true God is Father, Son and Holy Spirit.

The Christian concept could not have been invented by man. The ancient civilizations had a trinity of father-god, mother-goddess and their son-god. The Christian doctrine states that three persons are actually One God. A multiplicity of gods would cause dissension, as the Qur'an points out (17:42; 23:91).

THE TRINITY AND THE QUR'AN

There are two aspects of the *Qur'an*'s attitude to the Trinity. The factual attitude implies the Trinity, while the dogmatic attitude adheres to the rigid unity of God. Further, the *Qur'an* does not deal with the Biblical doctrine of the Trinity, but with the trinity of heretical sects.

The Qur'anic dogma says: "He is the God, the One, the eternal God, he has not begotten, nor has been begotten, and there is none equal to him" (112:1-4). The statement is final and decisive. God is not one of three. "Do not say three, desist, it is for your good: God is only One" (4:171). "They have disbelieved (blasphemed) who said that God is a third of three: there is no God but One God" (5:73). The Trinity was said to be of God, Mary and Jesus, according to an Eastern heretical sect. The Biblical concept of the Trinity is never mentioned directly in the dogmatic statements of the *Qur'an*. There was no awareness of the doctrine. If you were to ask, what is the Biblical doctrine of the Trinity according to the Qur'anic understanding of the doctrine? the answer will have to be, it is non-existent, but there is a dogmatic statement against the heretical doctrines of the Trinity.

THE STATUS OF JESUS

If the *Qur'an* is read by one who never read the *Bible* nor heard of the incarnation, the reader may not deduce that the doctrine exists, though it is implied. Two erroneous concepts are dealt with: natural generation and adoptionism.

The natural generation concept is that God actually begat Jesus as a man begets a son. "The Creator of the heavens and earth, how should he have a son when he had no consort?" (6:101); and "he, exalted the majesty of our Lord, has not taken a consort, nor a son" (72:3). The *Qur'an* denounces the claim that Christ is the son of God because it regards a son as a result of procreation. The Bible teaches incarnation.

The denunciation of the Adoptionist view is that God has not taken to himself a son: "And they said, God has taken to himself a son" (2:116;

10:68; 18:4; 19:35; 21:26; 23:91; 72:3). The verses use the same Arabic word for "taken to himself." It means, made his own, or adopted as his own property or creed or objective. This is clarified in 5:116, which says, "Did you say to men, take me and my mother as gods apart from God?" The taking is not the mere taking of a book or object, but the taking of the principles of the book as one's own. It is like one who becomes a citizen of a country other than his own. The implication is that God had no special relationship to Jesus by right, nor did he adopt him.

The Ebionites of the first century believed that Jesus was only a prophet in the line of the other prophets and the natural son of Joseph.[1] The Adoptionists of the late second century modified the view and said that Jesus was a perfect man who was adopted by God as his son and raised to the level of the Godhead.[2,3] The doctrine persists in Unitarianism. It is not the *New Testament* view of Jesus, and was regarded as heretical by the bishops who met at the Council of Nicaea in 325 A.D.

The implication of Adoptionism is that Jesus came into existence when he was conceived of Mary. The *Qur'an* rejects the Adoptionist view, but says in its own way that Jesus came into being at his conception. There is no indication of his pre-existence. What can we deduce from the factual statements of the *Qur'an*?

Mary's Purification

"O Mary, God has chosen you and purified you above all women" (3:42). The purification was not ceremonial or a ritual washing, but the preparation of Mary by God to make her fit to carry his word placed within her through his Spirit: "The Holy Spirit shall come upon you and the power of the highest shall overshadow you, therefore also that holy thing which shall be born of you shall be called the Son of God" (Lk.1:35; Mt.1:20). No such purification was done with the wife of Zechariah when she conceived with John (Yahya) (19:7). We have no right to neglect the significance of Mary's purification. It was necessary for the bearing of a sinless child.

Jesus, The Word of God Personified

"The angels said, O Mary, surely God gives you good news of a word from him, his name is Christ Jesus, the son of Mary. Highly honoured shall he be in this world and the next; near stationed to God" (3:45).

The word which was given to Mary was not the good news. The good news was about the word that had the personal name of Jesus. Jesus is identified with the word, or the word is personified in Jesus. Jesus is the word of God. Words express the thoughts and inward being of a person. Like actions, they reveal what the person is like. If someone talks sense, you say he is sensible, wise. If he talks foolishly, you say he is foolish. It is the same with God. His word expresses his personality. Thus, Jesus is the "brightness of his (God's) glory, and the express image of his person" (Heb.1:3). He is like God, that is he is God. The *Gospel* rightly says: "In the beginning was the Word, and the Word was with God, and the Word was God" (Jn.1:1). The word of God, the expression of his being is as eternal as he is, because it is part of him and is inseparable from him. The *Qur'an* emphasizes the personality of the word by saying that he is "the messenger of God AND a word from him" (4:171). The word is distinguished from God only this once in the *Qur'an.* Elsewhere, it says the "word of your Lord" (6:115; 11:119), or "a word that proceeds from your Lord" (11:110; 20:129; 41:45; 37:171), or similar. But in the case of Jesus, the *Qur'an* speaks of God and his word, making a distinction between one and the other. It gives the word a personal identity. Since the word of God is inseparable from him and is identified with the Jesus of history, then Jesus is the incarnation of the word.

God performs his deeds through his word. "He says and it is" (3:47,59). His word creates and therefore is not created. The *Gospel* is logical in saying of Jesus: "All things were made by him, and without him was not anything made that was made" (Jn.1:3). "By him were all things created" (Col.1:16). This is the implication that Jesus is the word of God. It means he is the same as God, that is God, and if he is God then he is a person and not a thing or an idea.

Committed To Mary

"Surely Christ Jesus the son of Mary is the messenger of God and a word from him which he placed within Mary, and a spirit from him" (4:171). The word was laid within Mary, not upon her, nor a word spoken to her. Mary said, "My Lord, how can I have a son seeing no mortal has touched me?" (3:47). Mary's question was a response to the angel's proclamation of the good news of a word whose name is Jesus. She understood that the word was to be a son within her womb, without the agency of a man. How do you explain such a thing? There is no adequate explanation to this amazing event apart from the incarnation. The incarnation means that the eternal, pre-existent word of God put on human flesh and became a man named Jesus: "And the Word was made flesh and dwelt among us and we beheld his glory, the glory as of the only of the begotten of the Father, full of grace and truth" (Jn.1:14).

The *Qur'an* explains the conception of Jesus as being similar to the creation of Adam. God said "be and he shall be" (3:59). But this is not how it happened. Adam was created of clay when there was no man on the earth. The generations of man came through the process of sexual reproduction. God had completed his creation and settled upon the throne (7:54; 20:5). Why did he break his law of procreation in the case of Jesus only? Muslims have a duty to answer this question, because the *Qur'an* states the event. Muslim commentators pass over the verses quickly. A unique event must have a unique significance. No other explanation than the incarnation of the word of God is possible. The *Qur'an* acknowledges that Jesus is a special person. He is also called a spirit from God, and the Spirit of God in the *Hadith*.[1] As soon as his conception was announced to Mary, the angel added that he will be notable and of a high estate in this world and the next (3:45).

Body and Spirit

Jesus is called the son of Mary in the *Qur'an*. He called himself the Son of man. The *Qur'an* and the *Bible* confirm his humanity by his title. His body was not divine or eternal, but was made immortal after his resurrection from the dead. "A body you have prepared for me" (Heb.10:5) expresses the matter well. Divinity cannot be made human, nor can it be destroyed. Jesus was human and divine at the same time: the God-Man, two natures in one person, as man is body and spirit. But the Holy Spirit was not the spirit of Jesus as the spirit of man is to man. This would have confined the Holy Spirit in a human body.

THE QUR'AN AND THE SPIRIT OF GOD

There are verses in the *Qur'an* in which the word spirit refers to the angel Gabriel. "And we sent to her our spirit, and he presented to her as a man without fault" (19:17) tells of the angel Gabriel appearing to Mary. The *Qur'an* was "brought down by the faithful spirit" (26:192-195). There are other verses that cannot apply to the angel. When God created Adam, "he breathed into him of his Spirit" (32:9), not of his Gabriel. He said to the angels to bow to him "when I fashion him and breathe of my Spirit into him" (15:28,29; 38:72). The Spirit of God gave life to Adam, not the angel Gabriel who is a created being. God has not delegated the act of creation to his creatures.

The Spirit of God is God. He is the life-giver. He cannot be less than God, otherwise God is less than himself. All the divine attributes which apply to God apply to his Spirit, of which we have to note personality and eternity. If God is a person, so is his Spirit.

You may say I am making two persons out of one. It is God who says, *My* Spirit. His Spirit is not his will, because he did not breathe of his will into Adam. God is a unified being, and his faculties and attributes are not divided. He acts as One, with all his faculties. His will does not act separately from his reason or his power. We cannot understand the nature of the matter, because we think of two persons as being separate individuals. There is no adequate human concept or word or example or parable or likeness to describe the tri-personality and yet the unity of God. Nor can the human mind understand it. God states the facts without explanation. It would be futile for him to explain.

REVELATION OF THE TRIUNITY OF GOD

There are indications in the *Old Testament* that God is more than one Person. He said: "Let us make man in our image, after our likeness" (Gen.1:26). The plural is not the plural of respect or kingship. God never referred to himself in the plural. He said, "I am the Lord," never "we are the Lord," or "we command you," or "obey us." But when he communed with himself regarding the creation of man, he said: "Let us." He gave an insight into his being. The opening verses of the Bible describe the creation. God is mentioned, and so is his Spirit. He spoke and it was done. The triune God acted in the creation of the world. The Spirit of God is mentioned frequently in the *Old Testament*, the Son is mentioned in Psalm 2, and the two Lords of David in Psalm 110. But, by and large, the unity of God is emphasized in the *Old Testament*: "Hear, O Israel: the Lord our God is One Lord" (Deut.6:4).

The Triunity or Trinity of God flowers in the *New Testament*, not as a doctrine to be learnt, but as a practical outworking of the plan of God in redemption. The Father sent the Son, the Son died for the world, and the Spirit makes effective the benefits of his death by the regeneration of sinners. Without the Trinity, there would be no redemption, and all men would be lost for ever. God could not hold the heavens and earth, and die at the same time. The Son died, not the Father nor the Spirit.

Have you ever considered that the disciples and apostles of Christ were Jews, whose banner in a heathen world was the unity of God? Why did they accept the triunity of God? The answer is that they saw the work of the triune God in their midst. They knew God, and Jesus spoke of his Father in heaven. They lived with Jesus, heard his words and claims, saw his works and life, and that he had the authority of God in himself. He asked them, "Whom do you say I am?" They said, "You are the Christ, the Son of the living God" (Mt.16:16). There was no other conclusion for them.

The Holy Spirit descended on them on the day of Pentecost, and they were filled with power. They preached Christ and did wonders. The disciples experienced the triune God and saw him at work in the salvation of the world. There was no need to convince them of the Trinity of God. Jesus sent them to preach to the nations and baptize them "in the name of the Father and of the Son and of the Holy Spirit" (Mt.28:19), not in the names in the plural. The Father, the Son and the Holy Spirit have one name for they are One.

DID JESUS CLAIM TO BE THE SON OF GOD?

It is commonly believed by Muslims that Jesus never claimed to be the son of God. This is not true.

Jesus identified himself with the Father: "I and my Father are one" (Jn.10:30). He accepted the title of the Son of God (Mt.16:16-20; Jn.11:27). When men asked whether he was "the Son of the Blessed," he answered, "I am, and you shall see the Son of man sitting on the right hand of power and coming in the clouds of heaven" (Mk.14:61,62; Lk.22:70,71). The Jews understood that he made himself equal with God, and said that he blasphemed.

Jesus referred to himself as the Son of God when he talked with Nicodemus (Jn.3:16-19), when he raised Lazarus (Jn.11:4), when he addressed the blind man to whom he had restored sight (Jn.9:35-37) and when he prayed to the Father (Jn.17:1). He claimed that the Father committed to him the resurrection of the dead, the judgment day and the giving of life to the spiritually dead (Jn.5:17-35). He claimed equal honour with God in verse 23: "All men should honour the Son even as they honour the Father." After a long discussion with the Jews on one occasion, he said to them, "Do you say of him whom the Father has sanctified and sent into the world, you blaspheme, because I said I am the Son of God?" (Jn.10:36).

It should not be thought that Jesus is begotten of the Father as a human father begets a son. When it says of God in the *Qur'an* that "he has not begotten, nor has been begotten, and there is no equal to him," it means the begetting of regeneration as in human life. Jesus was begotten as God begets his word and his mind begets his thoughts. The Father did not give life to Jesus, for he is life in the Godhead even as the Father is life and the Spirit is life. He said, "Before Abraham was, I am" (Jn.8:58), and prayed: "O Father, glorify me with your own self with the glory which I had with you before the world was" (Jn.17:5). His relationship with the Father is from eternity. There was no time when He was not the Son or was not in being. The generation of the Son from the Father, and the procession of the Spirit from the Father and the Son, is a description of the flowering of the exuberant life of God into three persons.

SUMMARY

The doctrine of the Trinity does not deny the Oneness of God. It is a further revelation of the mode of existence of God as Father, Son and Holy Spirit—one God, indivisible, eternal, so that God is not one without the other, yet each possesses the full attributes of God. The Father generates the Son from eternity as the mind of God generates his Word, while the Father and the Son give procession to the Holy Spirit as the mind and Word of God give procession to his will. The persons in the divine Trinity are co-equal, co-eternal and unfragmented.

The doctrine is denied by the *Qur'an*, which asserts the absolute unity of God. This unity is affirmed in the *Bible*. As God is One God, he is the Father, Son and Holy Spirit, of one name and substance. The *Qur'an* calls Jesus the Word of God and calls the Word Jesus, thus personifying the Word who, from eternity, is God. The eternal Word was laid within Mary to be born a baby, with a pure and sinless nature, through the process of incarnation. The Word was clothed in human flesh to effect the salvation of the lost. God acts as the triune God in creation, preservation and redemption. The *Qur'an* identifies the person of the Spirit of God from the person of God when it uses the term "my Spirit." The Spirit stands in the Godhead as does the Son in eternal triunity.

References

1. Al-Bukhari, vol.6, p.21.
2. A.R. Whitham, *The History of the Christian Church,* Rivingtons, London, 1924), p.99.
3. Kenneth Scott Latourette, *A History of Christianity,* (Eyre and Spottiswoode, Limited, London, 1955), p.121.
4. Whitham, *op. cit.*, p.145.
   Latourette, *op. cit.*, pp.143,144.

Chapter Ten

The Doctrine of Man—An Exposition of the Cow, Surah 2:30-38, in Conjunction with 7:10-15 and 20:115-126

"And when your Lord said to the angels, I am making a viceroy (khalifah) in the earth, they said, what, will you make in it one who will do corruption there, and shed blood, while we proclaim your praise and call you holy? He said, assuredly, I know what you know not. And he taught Adam the names, all of them; then he presented them to the angels and said, tell me the names if you are truthful. They said, praise be to you we know not save what you taught us, surely you are the knowing, the wise. He said, Adam, tell them their names. And when he told them their names, he said, did I not tell you I know the unseen things of the heavens and earth, and I know what things you reveal and what things you are hiding? And when we said to the angels, prostrate yourselves to Adam, so they prostrated themselves, save Iblis; he refused and waxed proud, and so became one of the unbelievers. And we said to Adam, dwell and your wife in the garden, and eat plentifully where you desire, but do not draw nigh this tree, lest you be of the wrongdoers. Then Satan caused them to slip therefrom and brought them out of what they were in. And we said, get you down, each of you an enemy of each; and in the earth a fixed place shall be yours and enjoyment for a while. Thereafter Adam received words from his Lord, and he turned towards him: truly he turns and is merciful. We said, get you down out of it, all together yet there shall come to you guidance from me, and whosoever follows my guidance, no fear shall be on them, neither shall they sorrow" (2:30-38).

INTRODUCTION

This passage is basic to the understanding of true religion. It is a mighty ocean into which the unwary sink. Traditional interpretation is linked to tales which show the fruitfulness of man's imagination. This is easily seen in any Arabic commentary on the *Qur'an*. The doctrine of man remains confused in the minds of Muslims because of a failure to understand what happened at the beginning of time. Men who lose the beginning can never catch up with it, despite intelligent efforts to do so. If the first premise of theology is false, then all that follows is also false.

How many people see that the passages under study teach clearly and unequivocally that man fell from the primary state in which he was created? Do they see that he is bound with fetters too great for him to unloose? There are those who have banished reason and praised Adam for allowing humanity to go through the throes of evil and come out victorious.[1,2]

The doctrine of Origins is taught here. The teaching of the *Qur'an* must be seen through its light. Subsequent theology must be based upon what happened initially. Without this, we end up with speculations about the course of human experience. We become bogged down by external forms of religion which lack substance and cannot give peace to the soul.

THE SOVEREIGNTY OF GOD

"Your Lord said to the angels, I am making a khalifah." It was the prerogative of God to do what pleased him. He did not consult the angels, but told them of his decision to create. He also graded the creation and made man his highest order. He decided that man should administer the world as khalifah. God knew what would befall man, because he created him. All was in his sovereign will and plan.

THE KHALIFATE OF ADAM AND HIS PROGENY

The subject is of such importance that no book written by Muslim writers about man fails to discuss it in some detail. The word "khalifah" has caused confusion with respect to its meaning. No one denies that the khalifah was the temporal ruler of Muslims after Muhammad. *Lisan ul-Arab*, or tongue of the Arabs, the expansive dictionary of the Arabic language, and the dictionary of *al-Fairuz Abadi* define khalifah as one who follows his predecessor and takes his place. The successor usually follows someone who dies or abdicates. Death is not involved here, for if Adam was the khalifah of God, it cannot be said that God died.

Since there was no man for Adam to succeed, the tales appeared. One is invariably told in the Arabic commentaries. Once upon a time, a race of Jinn or Genii inhabited the earth. They did wickedness and shed blood. God punished them through Satan, who lead a mighty army of angels and triumphed. The Jinn were scattered to the tops of the mountains and to the far islands of the sea. Thus banished, God gave the earth to another, that is Adam. Adam was thus the khalifah of the Jinn, a preposterous idea. It is unacceptable to make the *Qur'an* the basis for fairy tales.

Some commentators restricted the khalifate to Adam and the prophets. This view is incorrect. Hood was sent to the people of Ad, who remained unbelievers and said to them: "Remember that he appointed you khalifahs after the people of Noah" (7:69). They lived after Noah and were called khalifahs after him, though they were destroyed for their iniquity.

Verse 6:165 demolishes the idea that a select group is meant. It addresses all men, saying: "He who appointed you khalifahs in the earth." Muhammad's generation were appointed after their predecessors (10:14). "We delivered him and those with him in the ark and we appointed them khalifahs" (10:73) refers to Noah and his family. Noah is not singled out. His wife and children and their wives were included. They were the remnants of mankind, that is the whole of mankind. Some verses refer to those who do good works (24:55). The khalifate thus refers to believers and unbelievers, to prophets and ordinary people, and to those whom God destroyed for their sin. In short, it refers to Adam and his progeny.

THE FUNCTION OF THE KHALIFAH

God said to David: "We made you a khalifah in the earth, so judge between the people in truth" (38:26). David was given a charge over others as keeper, protector, warden and caretaker to work out justice and truth in God's name. Muhammad's early khalifahs completed what he began. They did not embark on a new course. Adam's khalifate does not mean that God abdicated his responsibility toward the earth. God subjected to him the sun and moon (14:33), the night and day (16:12), the clouds, rain, wind, rivers and seas: "Do you not see that God subjected to you what is in heaven and upon earth?" (31:20; 45:12,13; 22:65; 14:32). Having done that, he set man in charge of the earth. It is as if the lord of the house went on a journey and left his servant in charge of his household. The *Qur'an* supports this idea. God "created the heavens and the earth in six days then settled upon the throne" (7:54). We read: "It is he who created for you all that is in the earth then he lifted himself to heaven" (2:29), immediately before "I am making a khalifah." It is as if God finished his direct work and decided to work through the agency of men. The concept of stewardship, representation and viceregency is fully justified by the *Qur'an*.

THE TRUST OF THE CONFEDERATES, 33:72

Whenever the question of the khalifate of man is discussed, the concept of the Trust is linked with it. "We offered the trust to the heavens and the earth and the mountains, but they refused to carry it and were afraid of it, and man carried it; surely he was oppressive and ignorant."

Commentaries such as those by ar-Razi, al-Qurtubi, ibn Katheer, al-Jaleelain, Sayyed Qutub and others, explain the various meanings of the word. They quote those who said that it meant obedience, or the performance of religious duties, or washing after sexual intercourse, or for a woman to keep her sexual parts in the right way. Others said that God created the external sexual organs of man first of all, and that man must not abuse them. Others said it meant the ear, or the eye, or the leg or the arm. Anything that entered the fancy of men was included.

None of these explanations is tenable. God did not offer the heavens and earth and mountains the keeping of sexual parts, or arms, legs, or ears. Nor did he ask them to pray and fast, but they refused. The verse is written in this form to emphasize the role of man in the matter. The latest fashion in interpretation is that the trust is free will.[3,4] Only man could determine his destiny. No other, not even the angels, possessed a free will. Armed with this freedom, man went through hardship and disobedience in order to achieve godliness. We thus see the death of reason.

The Meaning of the Trust

The heavens, earth and mountains could not be said to choose. God deemed they were unable to carry the trust. Only one creature could, and that was man. He was the acme of God's creation. The protagonists of free will say that man's acceptance was voluntary. But for him to choose to accept meant that he had the capacity for choice in the first place. Their argument is circular and meaningless: man must possess freedom in order to choose to possess it. Having possessed it, he can choose whether to accept it or not. The main objection to their argument is the implication that God created an incomplete being; however, the will is part of the personality. Man did not carry part of his soul upon his shoulders. The trust was placed upon him. The verse does not even say that he was offered the option of carrying it. The only explanation of the trust is the khalifate—for which man was made and not consulted.

The Angels and Free Will

In order to magnify themselves, men deprived the angels of free will—without which they can be seen as robots or machines programmed to carry out certain functions.[5,6] A man can be "brain-washed" to be the same. This is the implication of obedience without freedom. The very idea is an invention of men. The *Qur'an* says that the angels are messengers of God who bring the truth to the prophets (35:1; 15:8). They praise God (39:75; 42:5), do not disobey him (66:6), and are not proud (16:49). If a young man is obedient to his parents, does it mean that he cannot disobey? If a man is law-abiding, is he incapable of breaking the law? A statement of fact does not negate its opposite. When the *Qur'an* says that the angels obey God, it makes a statement. It does not say they are compelled to obey, or have no free will to do otherwise. The argument equates obedience with the absence of free will. Free will must then be equated with disobedience. Adam was therefore incapable of obedience, or rather that his freedom in fact shackled him. It also means that the people in the garden have no free will, and are less than they were on earth. If they have free will, then they will choose to disobey God in the garden. The garden will be like the chaos of earth. The whole argument is a great fallacy. The angels obey God willingly, out of love and respect for him. Imagine God being surrounded by beings who have no choice but to praise him. He would be like the tyrant who forces people on the streets to cheer him. Blind obedience does not require understanding. The angels enquired of God about the khalifah, and questioned the wisdom of his action.

THE BIBLICAL CONCEPT OF THE KHALIFAH

Muslims think that the concept of the Khalifah is unique to the *Qur'an*. It is, in fact, enunciated in the first chapter of the *Bible*. God blessed our first parents and said to them: "Be fruitful and multiply and replenish the earth and subdue it: and have dominion over the fish of the sea and over the fowl of the air and over every living thing that moves upon the earth" (Gen.1:28). Man's dominion over the earth was established with the subjugation of all things to him. Genesis, Chapter 3, tells of his fall.

THE NATURE OF MAN WHEN HE WAS CREATED

"I am making a khalifah." A man does not send an animal to the bank to perform a transaction on his behalf. A policeman, not an industrialist, heads the police department. Similarly, God does not appoint a lion or a dog to be the steward of the earth. He appoints someone with a nature which resembles his own, and with qualifications necessary for the task. Adam had to be created in the likeness of God.

Adam was created a soul. "I am making a human of clay; when I have shaped him and breathed of my Spirit into him, fall down bowing to him" (38:71,72; 32:9; 15:29). The pinnacle of God's creation was not created by a word, but by a process. He was made alive and given a spirit by God's Spirit.

Adam's body was material. It could be seen and handled. His spirit was invisible, but appeared in his personality. Without his spirit Adam would have been like an animal. With his spirit, his thoughts went beyond himself to God. A dog may dream, recognize its master, be loyal and brave—but it does not comprehend loyalty, courage, justice, honour and the like. Such matters belong to man. They cannot be seen or weighed. They belong to the spirit of man. We must examine the features which made Adam a suitable steward of his creator.

THE SPECIAL FEATURES OF ADAM

Personality

The properties of personality are: reason, will, and natural affections or desires. These three faculties are bound together by the conscience as a matrix or mode of their existence.

Conscience does not exist separately. It is the guardian of the reason and the will, like a referee or probation officer. The desires are regulated through it to obey the will, which in turn listens to the dictates of reason. Conscience tries to ensure that the will performs what reason orders.

Reason is self-awareness and the ability to look at things objectively. It thinks a matter out, assesses the facts, and makes a judgment while the conscience is watching. The will should obey. If it tends to swerve under the influence of desires, the conscience tries to bring it back. Reason told Adam to obey God. The desire for knowledge swayed his will away from giving the obedience that reason demanded. His conscience failed to influence the outcome, but caused him to feel guilt. Animals do not act consciously or conscientiously. They live by instinct. The human baby does the same, but possesses the elements of the personality which flower with the passage of time.

The will is the ability of the soul to choose and to carry out its choice. Ability is necessary for the will to be free. The will is not the desire to do something. A man with a paralyzed arm may desire to move it, but he cannot. His will, deprived of ability, cannot be said to be free. Adam's will was free. It could offer obedience to God. Herein is the basis of moral responsibility. Adam's freedom placed the burden of responsibility upon his soul. When he disobeyed, his guilt was his alone. God was not the originator of his sin.

Desires are not under the control of the will. A hungry man cannot, by his will, remove his desire for food. The will to remain chaste does not remove the desire to be wanton. The desires influence the will to disobey reason. They are based upon the nature of man.

Morality

Morality indicates the moral nature. It has to do with actions and their governing principles. Many think that man is neutral in his moral nature. His behaviour, it is said, is learnt. Such statements are meaningless. The moral nature exists, therefore it must be positive. Neutrality or inertness of the moral nature is impossible. Animals do not have a moral nature, and are not morally responsible for their actions. The moral nature of Adam was derived from the nature of God. God is not neutral but good. He expected obedience from Adam. The parameters of morality are absolute. Indifference or neutrality is disobedience. Obedience is good; disobedience is evil. Both are moral traits. There is no neutrality here. A moral deed cannot be seventy percent good and thirty percent bad. There is no such division in morality. A good deed is not evil at the same time.

What was the moral nature of Adam? Was it good or was it evil? Those who say that Adam was created with both good and evil within him do not comprehend the nature of morality. If God placed evil within Adam, then God has evil within him. He can oppress and lie and deceive and cheat. The idea is blasphemous and monstrous. A holy creator could not produce anything but perfection.

Adam was better than the angels. God said to the angels, "Prostrate yourselves to Adam." The lesser bow to the greater, the servant to the master, and the humble citizen to the ruler. Adam was therefore greater than the angels. Will God ask the holy angels to prostrate themselves to an evil being? "We indeed created man in the fairest manner" (95:4).

The devil refused to bow to Adam and said: "I am better than he: you created me of fire and created him of clay" (7:12; 38:76). Fire burns clay, therefore the devil thought he was better than Adam. But Adam was clay moulded by the hand of God, his spirit created by the Spirit of God. The devil did not take account of Adam's spirit, which made his clay better than fire. It was the breath of God that made Adam higher than the angels. He was created complete, with a holiness that involved the whole of his being.

Knowledge

"And he taught Adam the names, all of them, and presented them to the angels." To name an object correctly requires a knowledge of its properties. Names originally described a notable feature of the named. Ishmael meant "may God hear." El was the ancient Semitic name for God. Bethel is the house of God. 'Ali is one who is high and exalted. Slater is one who slates, Baker one who bakes. For Adam to learn the names meant that he had a good memory tied up with a good intellect and reason.

What names did Adam learn? Some suggested the names of God. This is incorrect, for God presented the named to the angels. The angels knew the names of God. How could they call him holy, unless they knew his name to be holy? Some have suggested the names of the angels. This is not tenable, seeing that the named were presented to the angels. Others have suggested the names of Adam's progeny. This is not tenable either, for Adam's progeny had not been born. What was it that was mobile and which the angels had not seen before? It was not the lake, mountain, river, flowers or heavenly bodies. The most likely reference was to the land animals. The angels had not seen the lion, the bear, and the horse. They had no idea what they were. How could they name them? That Adam could repeat the names to the angels meant that he had a memory which retained the knowledge he learnt.

Spirituality

This means that Adam was able to know God. The basis was his creation of the Spirit of God. Adam's spirit responded to the Spirit of God. God befriended him, showed him the animals, and taught him their names. He then took him to the angels and presented him to them. If we were to use human terms, we would say that God was proud of Adam. He was as near to God as the angels, if not nearer. He differed, by his spirituality, from the animals. Man cannot commune with a dog or a cat at the same level as with a man. Spirit must commune with a kindred spirit. Adam communed with God because he had something in common with him. Because of Adam's spirituality, his loyalty had to be tested.

Potential Immortality

The heading may appear strange because Adam has been long dead. What is meant is that God did not place the seed of death in him. If Adam had been created mortal he would have been imperfect and lower than the angels. For Adam to die required the element of corruption and degeneration in his newly created nature. A dead Adam is lesser than the clay. His stench is unbearable. Imagine God gathering the angels quickly and saying to them: "Come, angels, prostrate yourselves to Adam. Hurry, before he becomes a stinking mass, a putrefying lump!"

SUMMARY

It pleased God to create Adam as his khalifah, or steward, upon earth. God made him, through this office, master of the earth to work justice and equity in his name. Adam was endowed with qualities which made him fit for the task. The foundation of these qualities was the mode of his creation—of clay, made alive by the Spirit of God. Adam therefore received qualities which belonged to God in an absolute manner. The qualities were a personality with reason, will and holy desires, a moral nature, knowledge, spirituality and potential immortality. Adam could not have responded to his maker if this had not been the case. Without such qualities he would have been no better than any animal. The communication of the divine qualities made Adam capable of befriending God. Yet he was not divine. His qualities depended upon God and could be lost or debased if they were not confirmed in holiness. This happened when he sinned.

References

1. Aisha Adb ur-Rhaman, Al-Qur'an wa qadaya el-Insan, p.36,37,74.
2. Hasan Sa'b, Al-Islam wal-Insan, (Dar ul-'Ilm-lil-Malayeen, Beruit, 1981), pp.86-88.
3. Aisha Abd ur-Rahman, p.72
4. Hasan Sa'b p.86.
5. Aisha Abd ur-Rahman, p.34.
6. As-Sayyed Sabeq, Al'aqa-id-el-Islamiyyat, (Dar ul-Kitab el-Arabi, Beirut, 1985), p. 114.

Chapter Eleven
The Doctrine of Man Continued—The Fall

THE PROHIBITION

"And we said, Adam dwell and your wife in the garden and eat thereof plentifully as you desire, but draw not nigh to this tree, lest you be of the wrongdoers" (2:35; 7:19). "And we made a covenant with Adam, but he forgot and we found in him no resolve" (20:115).

The Prohibition was not a covenant between two parties in the same sense as a contract. God gave the order, and Adam had to obey.

Adam and his wife were moral beings, with an obligation to live as God demanded. This meant willing obedience, by which their friendship with God would be secured. They were in a state of probation from which they could lapse. They were given the opportunity to make their uprightness evident by action, rather than remaining dormant; they had to respond to God sooner or later. It is like a man who proves his faithfulness to his wife at a time when he could be unfaithful, or like a child who jumps into his father's arms without fear.

"Do not approach this tree" is a negative command which required a positive action. The command was associated with a threat. This means that Adam and Eve had knowledge of right and wrong. That they understood that punishment would follow meant that they had a sense of justice. The moral obligation was theirs with its rewards and punishment. If they did not have a sense of responsibility, the trial would have been futile, and their punishment for disobedience would have been unjust. Obedience would have been rewarded with blessings.

The threat was expulsion from the garden into a life of hardship. "Lest you be of the wrongdoers"; "let him not expel you from the garden, so that you will suffer hardship. It is assuredly given to you neither to hunger, nor to suffer the sun" (20:117-119). The promise implied was the opposite of the threat.

The word translated to "wrongdoers" has the modern meaning of oppressors. It is derived from the Arabic root word "dhalama." It means he placed a thing in its wrong place, or the water reached the valley in a place where it did not reach before, or the earth was dug up in the wrong place. This is exactly the notion of sin, which is missing the mark.

The tree was not evil in itself. It became the test object when God willed to use it in this capacity. The sin was in the disobedience. Probation carried the possibility of a blessing. God did not encourage sin.

The devil's object was to discredit Adam through temptation. He wanted to get at God through his highest creature. Adam was holy and did not have evil thoughts toward God. The temptation came from outside of him: "Shall I point you to the tree of immortality and a kingdom that does not fade?" (20:120). Adam and his wife had the power to resist.

The tempter, Satan or Iblis, disobeyed God and was cursed: "Go out from hence; you are accursed. Upon you is the curse until the day of judgment: (15:34,35). He is called accursed in 3:36; 16:98; 38:77. He was already evil when he refused to bow down to Adam. He became evil through rebellion. God could have made Adam like him as a result of his sin, but he showed him mercy. Satan was not shown mercy and judgment awaits him. He became the arch-enemy of God and intended to pervert the whole of mankind. Yet our parents were tempted by God's leave. They listened to Satan's lies, ate of the tree and disobeyed God willingly and knowingly.

DID ADAM FORGET?

"He forgot and we found in him no constancy" (20:115).

Some say that Adam was not blameworthy because he forgot God's command.[1] They misinterpret the meaning of the *Qur'an*. We have seen that Adam had a fine memory, since he recited the names to the angels. When he said, "Do not draw nigh to *this* tree," God showed him the tree. Adam would have remembered it when he saw it again, especially since God attached a threat with the command. He could not say, "Oh, I thought it was that other tree!" We read in 20:126: "Our commandments came to you and you forgot them, so shall you be forgotten today." If Adam's memory was defective, then we have to attribute the same to

God. He said that he will forget Adam as Adam forgot his commandments. This interpretation is hideous. The meaning of forgot is "neglected," or "paid no heed," or "took no account." This is supported by the Arabic dictionary, *Lisan ul-Arab*. Adam showed neither determination nor constancy and disobeyed God. It is amazing that he was deceived, seeing that God warned him against Satan's wiles, saying, "Adam, surely this is an enemy to you and your wife, so let him not expel you both from the garden" (20:117). His punishment proved his guilt.

MAN'S RESPONSIBILITY

Although nothing happens without God's will, it is a gross error to justify Adam's sin. That would make God guilty. Man is judged according to his obedience or disobedience, not according to the secret will of God. You cannot kill a man and think that you fulfilled God's will. This is a perverse way of thinking. A man killed a child by his careless driving, and had the audacity to tell me that it was God's will. How easily do men blame God for their evil deeds! God warned and threatened Adam with punishment. Adam alone was responsible for his disobedience. The devil refuses to take the blame for his deception of mankind. He will say on the judgment day: "God promised you the truth and I promised you, then I failed you, for I had no authority over you but that I called you and you answered me. So do not blame me, but blame yourselves" (14:22). Is the devil more honest than some people? If you justify Adam, you justify the sinful deeds of all mankind.

A paragraph in the *Qur'an* may lead to misunderstanding. Moses of Israel walked with a man who showed him the futility of pride.[2] He killed a lad (18:74) and said, "his parents were believers, and he feared that he will weary them with evil and unbelief" (18:80). The man had a special knowledge of God's will (18:65); otherwise his deed would have been a terrible crime. No man may judge another by what he might become.

THE CONSEQUENCES OF THE SIN OF OUR FIRST PARENTS

This is the heart of the matter. It is the only explanation for the evil state of the world. It also lays down the foundation for what is required for our return to God.

Paradise Lost

"Get you down out of it" (2:36). The garden was no longer a fit place for sinners. Instead of elaborating upon the importance of this fact,

Muslim commentators become absorbed with trivial conjectures about what Adam found upon earth, and when and where he arrived, and in what posture he landed. They miss the point that Adam's sin drove him out of paradise. He lost the immediate friendship of God. "Their Lord called them" (7:22) as if from a distance.

Wretchedness

They ate in ease from the trees of the garden. They were "neither to hunger therein, nor to go naked, neither to thirst" (20:117-119). Later, they would suffer such hardship, and obtain their food and drink with wretchedness. Hunger, thirst and disease became their lot.

The Enmity of Nature

They will be hurt by the heat of the sun (20:119). All things were subjugated to them, but now, the sea would drown them and hurricanes would blow away their homes. Natural disasters are the result of sin.

Pollution of the Conscience

"And their shameful parts appeared and they took to stitching upon themselves leaves of the garden" (7:22; 20:121).

Nakedness was not shameful to them, for they were husband and wife. Their sin was not sexual; that was not possible between them. Why do you think the woman was called Adam's wife? They could not have been covered by animal skins, for that would have meant bloodshed in the garden. They became ashamed after their sin. Their guilty conscience made them feel unclean in their own eyes and in the eyes of God. They became fearful and said: "Our Lord, we have wronged ourselves" (7:23).

Corruption of the Moral Nature

"Will you set one therein who will do corruption in it?" "Get you down, each is an enemy of each" (2:30,36; 7:24; 20:123).

Enmity was not between Adam and his wife on the one hand and the devil on the other. The devil was already their enemy. God addressed Adam and his wife in 20:123 in the Arabic plural for two persons when he said, "Get down." There is more to this than meets the eye.

In what does enmity consist? Enmity is founded in selfishness, hatred, a desire to possess another's right, whether it be money, wife or country.

It involves lies, theft, murder, rape and the like. It ultimately involves death. Enmity does not always manifest itself in deeds. You may hate or envy a person without harming him. Such qualities became part of Adam's nature. You do not carry enmity in your pocket and take it out when you sleep. It is part of you. The nature of our first parents was corrupted from uprightness, holiness and purity.

Bloodshed

"Will you set therein one who will do corruption in it and shed blood, while we proclaim your praise and call you holy?" This was the angels' question to God. Some say that the angels attempted to get more information out of God by saying: "Will you make a bloodshedder?" God will answer, no, but a good fellow. This interpretation makes the angels twisters of tongues. They only knew what God told them: "We know not save what you have taught us" (2:32). God must have told them that Adam would shed blood and do corruption. They were amazed. The angels did not prostrate themselves to a corrupt man and a shedder of blood. The conclusion is inescapable: Adam became these things after his sin. Adam may not have shed human blood but probably shed animal blood. Bloodshed involves the element of violence, ugliness and horror. Imagine the hideousness of bloodshed in a newly-created world.

Corruption in the Earth

Corruption is based upon bloodshed and enmity. It involves a change in Adam's nature. Evil deeds of the moral, physical and spiritual types follow. Injustice and the destruction of life are involved. The earth is polluted and destroyed. Animals are terrorized and hunted for sport.

Death

"You will have in the earth an abiding place and enjoyment for a while." "He said, therein you shall live and therein you shall die" (2:36; 7:24,25).

The clarity with which these verses speak is undoubted. What is astounding is the failure of many to understand their meaning. That "for a while" means until the resurrection day is not acceptable, though it is mentioned in the *Hadith*.³ The words were spoken to Adam and his wife and applied to them. They were not spoken to their progeny. "For a while" means for a limited period—not forever, but for a time that will end. It must not be thought that after a while Adam and his wife were to be transported into outer space. It means they had to die. This is said distinctly in 7:25: "Therein you shall live and therein you shall die." Death involves the degeneration of the body, which will grow old and crumble beneath the weight of its years. All who praise Adam for his sin, take heed. Nothing uglier could have happened to one created of the Spirit of God and to whom, once upon a time, the angels prostrated themselves.

Spiritual Blindness

Adam's intimate relationship with God was lost. His nature was degraded. You may say, all is forgiven, come home again, Adam, for it says: "He turned towards him" (2:37). But the verse starts by saying: "And Adam received words from his Lord." He was reprimanded: "Did I not prohibit you from the tree and tell you, verily Satan is to you a manifest foe?" (7:22). The reprimand sufficed to bring a guilty conscience to see its guilt. Adam was polluted in all his faculties, including the realm of his spirit. He became spiritually dead, incapable of arriving at a knowledge of God without a word of reprimand or admonition. God took the initiative: "He said, get you down, both of you:" "Whosoever turns away from my remembrance, his life shall be of narrowness and on the resurrection day we shall raise him blind. He said, my Lord, why did you raise me blind when I was wont to see? He said, even so, our signs came to you and you neglected them, so today you are neglected" (20:122-126). Repentance followed the blame. "Yet there shall come to you guidance from me, and whosoever follows my guidance, no fear shall be upon them, neither shall they sorrow" (2:38). Guidance comes first, then the following. God is the head, the leader, not the tail or follower.

The Spoiling of the Khalifate

"We have offered the trust to the heavens and the earth and the mountains, but they refused to carry it, but man carried it: surely he was an evildoer and very ignorant" (33:72). Man made a mess of things. Instead of being the righteous guardian of the earth, he falls upon the creatures in his care. He slays them and eats their flesh. All nature is in havoc. The sun beats upon his head, the wind uproots his dwellings and crops, and the earth does not yield her strength. Man does not safeguard nature and its life, but exploits them unjustly.

SUMMARY

Adam was justly penalized for his wilful disobedience. He lost the pleasures of the garden and the intimate friendship of God. He suffered the degradation and degeneration of his physical nature, and the whole of creation was involved in this.

He became corrupt and a corrupter of the earth and a shedder of blood. His whole being was involved. He became spiritually blind, unable to know God without primary guidance from God. His khalifate was spoiled, and his life became subject to death.

DID ADAM'S SIN AFFECT HIS PROGENY?

The answer is definitely yes. Muslims write repeatedly in their commentaries and books that Adam sinned for himself alone. When he repented, the slate was wiped clean. This is a travesty of the truth. His progeny suffered all that he suffered, and therefore must have been involved in his sin.

Paradise Lost: None of us is born in the garden. Can you imagine a garden filled with evildoers?

Hardship of Life: The experience of all men. They starve in Africa and Asia. All fall victim to disease.

Enmity of Nature: Evident in the disasters of the wind and rain and hurricanes and floods and drought. Thousands are buried beneath the rubble of an earthquake, or flee from the fury of an erupting volcano.

Pollution of the Moral Nature: Who would dare to expose his thoughts for others to read? Who has a pure mind, undefiled by evil musings? Whose conscience does not know guilt? We all do what we know to be wrong.

Enmity: Describes the life of man precisely. It is the most notable feature of human existence. The division of historical periods, despite its artificiality, is based upon conquest or treaties after wars, or the assassination of some important person. Even in times of peace, man is afraid of his fellow. Countries build armaments of destruction. Young men are sent to their deaths in mortal combat at the whim of dictators. Selfishness abounds in the heart, with hatred, envy, lust and a desire to possess what belongs to another. Men possess other men's wives. The affections control them as they control a dog's behaviour.

Bloodshed: It underlies the history of man. Cain killed his brother out of jealousy. Wars are rampant in our century. Children are exposed to poisonous gas. So-called advanced nations have been as guilty as primitive savages.

> Millions fell to his bombs,
> To his swords and rockets;
> Heads were smashed, throats were cut;
> Eyes removed from sockets;
> But the sea and mountain,
> The free wind of the storm,
> Raged to claim a thousand
> Of life of every form.

Corruption in the Earth: This aspect of Adam's fall is seen in the accidental and wilful spillage of oils and harmful wastes into the oceans and rivers, and in the pollution of the atmosphere. Animals are hunted to extinction. The guardians of justice are its slayers. Lawyers are interested in winning a case, not in seeing that justice is done. No one cares to know that a man may be outraged because the law does not give him justice. Many buy their freedom when guilty. The strong devour the weak.

Death: The experience of all men. Congenital deformities and disease are part of the corruption of man's physical frame.

> However long they seem, few are the days of man;
> Death waits outside his home to shorten his life span;
> At times, it comes in peace; it knocks his wooden door;
> At times, in violence, slays him upon the floor.
> Men are one by nature: all men are born to die;
> Men are born to suffer; all men are born to cry.

Spiritual Darkness: The need of all men for the guidance of God. Tell men about God, and many will deny his existence. They think that their intellect forbids them to accept tales. The intellect of the meanest of men may cause him to be like-minded. The mind does not see the obvious. The genius in mathematics or physics may be a fool in spiritual things.

The Spoiling of the Khalifate: Earth at the brink of destruction. It works partly for man's good, and is often his enemy. Man inflicts hardship and death on creatures in his care. He is often the victim of things once subjugated to him. The shark eats him in the sea. Viruses and bacteria destroy his health and life. In short, man is not in control of the world; rather, he is often victim of powers and creatures which were once under the dominion of Adam.

WHY IS ADAM'S PROGENY INVOLVED IN HIS SIN?

It cannot be doubted that since we suffer what befell Adam, we must be tied with him somehow.

THE UNITY OF THE HUMAN RACE

"It is he who created you of one living soul and made of him his spouse" (7:189). "Mankind, fear your Lord who created you from a single soul and from it created its spouse and from the pair of them scattered abroad many men and women" (4:1).

The human race is related to Adam by direct descent. Even Adam's wife was not created in isolation, but from him. The continuity of the race was guaranteed by God. When he drowned the earth with a flood, he left a remnant for the repopulation of the planet. All men possess one nature, one sinfulness and are bound by the same law of God. God determined one way by which they may be redeemed from their sin.

Some regarded Adam as the tree which branched into his progeny. This is not true, in that Adam's soul cannot be said to be divided so that each human being receives part of it. One part of the soul does not go to heaven while the other perishes in hell. Another explanation is that God creates us individually with a sinful nature. This too is false, for God is not the author of sin in us. If we are created neutral, as some believe, then we have to explain why children die before they commit any sin. Death is a consequence of sin.

Imputation

Imputation is the only explanation for our involvement with Adam. It means the just and judicial laying of an offence or righteousness to the charge of another, whether the offence or righteousness belonged to that person or not. In the case of sin, it is the laying of Adam's sin to us. Each is regarded as having been tested and failed when Adam was tested and failed. This is because Adam was not the neutral head of the race, but its federal head and representative.

Adam as the Federal Head of the Human Race

Adam was not a mere individual under probation, but the sole representative of the human race. God has not created any of us with a holy nature, nor tested us as he tested him. Adam stood or fell on the behalf of his progeny.

The father represents the family, the parliament the nation; the Skaikh the tribe, and the ambassador his government. The unity of mankind is defined in a smaller context when an injury is done to one member of the family or tribe. It is as if the whole family or tribe was injured. This is the basis for vendetta. God treated the human race on the same principle, when there was one man in the earth. It is as if he said, "Obey me and you and your seed will be blessed; disobey, and you and your seed will be cursed." Moses said to Adam, according to the *Hadith*: "It is you who expelled mankind from the garden by your sin and brought upon them wretchedness."[4] Adam will say on the judgment day: "My Lord has been angry with a great anger the like of which has not been before and will not be thereafter. He forbade me the tree and I disobeyed him: my soul, my soul, my soul."[5] Representation should be clear to any Arab. It does no injustice to what the *Qur'an* teaches: "Whoso kills a soul, not to retaliate for a soul slain, nor for corruption done in the land, shall be as if he had slain mankind altogether" (5:32). But mankind came also from Adam's wife. She sinned when she ate of the tree.

Human Experience

There is no other explanation, however difficult it is to accept the doctrine of imputation. Why is there hatred, lust, envy, bloodshed, and sexual immorality within the heart? Why does a baby die before it has the chance to sin actively? Why are some born with an open back, or a defective brain? Is God unable to do a better job of his creation? Does he create by trial and error? Some say the afflictions of children are trials for the parents, so that they can draw closer to God. Since when have children been a sacrifice for their parents' welfare? Many will give their lives for their children and will reject God because of a mishap to them. Death and disease are a result of sin. Children are involved. Why did not God spare the infants when he drowned the earth with a flood, and destroyed the people of Lot or of Ad and Thamud? He destroyed the sinful race and its seed.

Adam Repented for Himself Alone

Adam's children were born of him after he sinned and became polluted by sin. His probation was on their behalf in his state of innocence. Each stands on his own merits after this. Adam repented for himself alone. He was no longer the representative of the race, but an individual who lost his exalted standing.

SUMMARY

Our first parents stood before God as the head of mankind to be tested on their behalf. They were mankind. When they fell, mankind fell. They became polluted in their personality. Their physical frame degenerated and died. They became shedders of blood and corrupters of an earth that was cursed because of them. Nature rose against them and their Khalifate was spoilt. Their progeny suffered the same fate because they were regarded as having been tested in their parents, who failed the trial on their behalf. Those who reject mankind's involvement in Adam's sin must explain why mankind suffered what he suffered. We have no right to reject facts even if we do not have the ultimate explanation for them.

References

1. As-Sayyed Sabeq, Al-'aqa-id el-Islamiyyat, p.184.
2. Al-Bukhari, vol.6, p.110-117.
3. Ibid., p.73.
4. Ibid., p.120,121.
5. Ibid., p.105,106.

Chapter Twelve

The Doctrine of Man Continued—Sin

THE NATURE OF GOD AND THE NATURE OF SIN

"And Adam disobeyed his Lord and erred" (sinned) (20:121).

How many books written by Muslims discuss or dedicate a chapter to the subject of sin? I have not seen one. In what does the nature of sin consist? It consists in the departure of the moral character from God's likeness. Notice that the nature of sin does not consist in doing or not doing things. If the moral character in man, which is part of his being, has departed from its likeness to the character of God, which is holiness, then man's character is sinful. Obedience or disobedience is how the character manifests itself. It has the standard of God's law as the reference. This is based upon the character of God. Departure from it, or disobedience, is sin. Adam listened to the insinuations of the devil and mistrusted God. He positively determined to disobey. He separated his will from God's will. The state of his soul gave rise to his actions.

Why does God command certain actions and forbids others? God's will is not arbitrary. It is based on his attributes. When he commands or forbids an action, it is because his nature demands it. It is easy to prove this. God does not love workers of corruption (2:205; 5:64; 28:77), because he is pure. He hates hypocrites (2:276) because he is honest, oppressors (3:57,140) because he is just, aggressors (2:190; 7:55) because he is not an aggressor, proud pretenders (4:36; 57:23) because he is not vain, evil words (4:148) because he is truthful, and traitors (8:58; 22:38) because he is faithful.

GOD'S NAMES TELL OF HIS NATURE

Some of God's names tell of his being, others of his deeds. God is One (2:163), the Singular, the Everlasting (112:1,2), the Knower of the unseen and the Witness, the Merciful, the Compassionate, the King, the Holy One, the Peaceable, the Faithful, the Preserver, the Powerful, the Compeller, the Sublime, the Creator, the Maker, the Shaper, the Mighty, the Wise, the Praised One (59:21-24; 62:1), the Distinguished and Glorious, the First and the Last, the Revealed and the Hidden (57:1-3), the High and Great (42:3,4), the Living and Self-Subsisting (2:255), the Embracing, the Rich, the Generous (2:115,263; 27:40), the Kind, the Aware (67:14), the Loving, the Forgiving (11:90; 85:14), the Giver of life and death (6:162), the Grasper and the Outspreader (2:245), the Numberer (36:12), the Truth (3:60), the Avenger (7:136), the Light (24:35), the Gatherer and Judge (3:9), the Guide and Destroyer (7:3,4; 11:87), the Hearing and Seeing One (42:11).

God is loving because he is Love, merciful because he is Mercy, the Avenger because he is just. He shows compassion because he is compassionate, requires holiness because he is Holy. It cannot be denied that his law is an expression of his nature. We must be like him: loving, kind, generous, merciful, compassionate, pure in heart and spirit, good, kind, truthful and just.

Some attributes belong to God alone. He only is the One Eternal, Everlasting, the First and the Last, the Light, the Giver of Life, the Almighty, the Creator, the Glorious, the Omnipresent, Omniscient and Omnipotent.

GOD'S HOLINESS

The angels said: "We proclaim your praise and extol your holiness" (2:30). Although God is all the magnificent things which are mentioned in the *Qur'an*, the angels do not extol his justice or mercy. It is his holiness which they magnify. It is because God's holiness pervades his nature, and through it, all his other attributes are shown. He is One, but the Holy One; Truth, but Holy Truth. He is Holy Power, Holy Justice, Holy Love, Holy Mercy, Holy Compassion, Holy Goodness. In short, he is glorious in Holiness (Ex.15:11). When God took an oath to establish David's Kingdom he said: "Once I have sworn by my Holiness, I will not lie unto David" (Ps.89:34,35). As the angels extol his holiness in the *Qur'an*, they do so in the *Bible*. They cover their faces in his presence and cry: "Holy, Holy, Holy is the Lord" (Is.6:2-4). He is the Light of the heavens and the earth (24:35). "In him is no darkness at all . . . no variableness neither shadow of turning" (1Jn.1:5; Jas.1:17). He is "of purer eyes than to behold evil and cannot look upon iniquity" (Hab.1:13). This is why he said: "Be ye holy for I am Holy" (Lev.19:2; 11:44,45).

THE STATE OF SIN

Do you see now that sin is not just a matter of doing or not doing certain things? As God is holy in his nature, so he expects holiness of nature from us. As holiness is the state in which God exists, sin is the state in which man exists since the fall of Adam. Adam was in a state of holiness at his creation. By state is meant the condition in which the soul is found. There is nothing more damning to men and women than to think that sin is a list of wrongs. Man commits sin because the driving principle of his life is his sinful nature. When Adam swerved from his loyalty to God, he disobeyed. He was not like someone who threw a ball or took off a shirt, but like someone who developed a blood disease, or a disease affecting his immune mechanism, or a skin with festering sores.

Consider Satan. When he refused to bow down to Adam, God said to him: "It is not for you to wax proud here, so go forth; surely you are among the humbled." He said, "Now, because you have perverted me [caused me to err or go astray], I will surely sit in ambush for them" (7:12-17). Satan was changed to a devil because of his pride. We see in him the reward of sin—total moral corruption and enmity against God. God decided to let him remain in his iniquity, but to save Adam. To say that God is good, Satan evil, and man a sinner in need of redemption, is to describe the state of each.

What is the driving force behind man's actions? It is the force of his moral character, or soul. When speaking of unbelievers, the *Qur'an* says: "It is not the eyes that are blind, but blind are the hearts within the breasts (22:46) . . . in their hearts is a sickness" (9:125; 24:50). Jesus said: "A good man out of the good treasure of his heart brings forth that which is good; and an evil man out of the evil treasure of his heart brings forth that which is evil" (Lk.6:45; Mt.12:35), "for out of the heart proceed evil thoughts, murders, adulteries, fornications, thefts, false witness, blasphemies" (Mt.15:19). God looks upon the state of the soul. A good deed is judged by whether it was done to please God or not. Many do not understand these vital issues, and so live a life of conceit.

God requires total obedience in heart and action, and a conformity to his law and nature. When Adam sinned he became corrupt. He alienated himself from God, whereas he once walked with his Creator. You may say that total obedience is not possible. This is so, but it is God's standard. God will not lower his standards lower than the lowest of men, so that they may fulfil his demands.

HOW IS MAN AFFECTED BY SIN?

That the nature of man is sinful is sufficiently evident to end all discussion. But from the practical aspect, each man has to find out for himself that he has not come up to God's demands. We have seen how Adam and his wife tried to cover their nakedness when their consciences became guilty as a result of their disobedience. Their sin defined their legal status before God: they were offenders. A sense of condemnation within them made them feel that they deserved punishment. But guilt is not only an obligation to satisfy justice. A man who pays a fine for an offence, or spends a term in jail, does not become innocent. His crime remains a blot upon his character. When a thief's hand is cut off, the mark of his punishment endures throughout his life. Others may be warned, but he is known to have stolen by all who see him. Justice obtains its right, but cannot remove the legal sense of guilt and make a guilty man just. Guilt is universal, whether it is acknowledged or not. The need for forgiveness is sufficient proof that all men are guilty.

There is another characteristic of sin and that is its polluting power. The mind is polluted so that it denies faith in God. It might even find it reasonable to take what it desires, such as another man's wife, or possessions, or life. The will follows the direction of unholy desires, rather than reason, when reason judges the wisdom of abstaining from an evil deed. The desires are unholy. The heart is not free from lust, jealousy, hatred and selfishness. If we examine our hearts and compare what we think and desire with what God demands, the truth of the matter becomes obvious.

The *Qur'an* describes the nature of man in sin. He is weak (4:28), oppressive and a wrongdoer (14:34; 42:48; 43:15), quarrelsome (16:4; 18:54; 36:77), hasty, excessively mean (17:11,100), ignorant (33:72), fretful, impatient with evil, grudging with good (70:19), ungrateful (100:6), a shedder of blood and a corrupt person (2:30). This was not the case of Adam when he was created, but what he and his progeny became.

THE DEGREES OF SIN

It is a lesser sin to steal than to kill, to lust than to commit fornication or adultery. All sins do not merit the same degree of punishment. A man may be fined or jailed for stealing, but his life is not forfeit. An eye for an eye, and a tooth for a tooth (Ex.21:24; surah 5:45) means that a man should not be killed for a lesser offence.

The gradation in punishment has led people to believe, when considering eternal issues, that some sins are more important than others. Religion has the dual function of organizing life on earth, and the greater function of preparing man for eternity. Gradation in punishment is relevant only to the former. It is a false notion to think that God will determine man's eternal destiny upon a division of his law. His law is one unit, despite its several parts. To break one commandment is to break the law. If a man drives through a red traffic signal, he does not break the law of the traffic signals, but the whole of the traffic law. He cannot plead that he stopped at all the previous signals and pedestrian crossings. God's law is an expression of himself, and if divided, it means that there is a division in God, that he is no longer One. Have you considered that all that our first parents did was to eat of a tree? Could there have been a smaller sin than this? Yet it brought upon them and their progeny destruction and death and banishment from the presence of God. If our parents failed in their state of innocence, how do you think you can please God with your own efforts in keeping his law?

THE PUNISHMENT OF SIN

There is much confusion about this subject. Society suffers from the effects of the confusion. Punishment may be negative or positive. A fine deprives a man from the free use of his money. Jail deprives him of his liberty; execution deprives him of his life. Community service is both negative and positive, as when man works against his desires and labours for others. Punishment implies responsibility for the offence. A just punishment gives an offender what he deserves. It is unjust to jail a man for a few years for committing the crime of murder. Injustice may drive men to rebel and seek justice by their own hand.

Some think that the object of punishment is to reform the criminal. This is a foolish notion, in that punishment does not change the nature of a man. When God sends a man to hell, he does not send him to a reform school. The real object of punishment is to satisfy the demands of justice. This is why justice must be seen to be done. God may punish men and women in this life, but his eternal punishment is uniform. It is the sending of the guilty to the abode of misery and suffering we call hell. There is no gradation in the degree of suffering in hell. The banishment from God is eternal. The least sin is worthy of hell since it flouts God's law. Since God demands absolute and total obedience, and since none of the progeny of Adam has been able to give it, all are condemned to hell. We need God to save us from this miserable destiny. God's justice must take its course. None will be saved unless God stretches out his hand and finds another way to satisfy his justice. He planned and carried out his plan of salvation in Jesus Christ.

THE GUIDANCE OF GOD

"Surely, there will come to you a guidance from me, and whoever follows my guidance no fear shall be upon them, neither shall they sorrow" (2:38).

Is man able to come to God without God's guidance in the first place? Spiritual death came as a result of sin. Guidance became necessary even for Adam, who knew God before his sin. The real question is whether man is able to change his character so that he will act differently from his basic nature. A man may sit or stand when he desires, but will he desire or be able to turn himself to love God without God's action upon his soul? Sin corrupted the whole nature of man. His mind, if left alone, will not seek God. His will cannot choose God, because it cannot decide upon what the mind does not perceive. His desire is not for God but for gratification of the demands of his nature.

CAN MAN CHANGE HIS NATURE?

"We created man in the fairest stature, then we restored him the lowest of the low, except for those who believed and did righteous deeds; they shall have a wage unfailing" (95:4-6). The verse is misinterpreted to mean that man is born good, and does evil when he grows up. This means that he is born a lamb and becomes a wolf. The truth is that man's nature flowers into sin when he is capable of showing his real self. It means that God created Adam good, but he became the lowest of the low. Such selfishness is seen in the child who will not share his toys with another.

You may say, "God will not change what is in a people until they change what is in themselves" (8:53; 13:11). The verse does not deal with the soul, nor with the individual, but with a group of people or a nation. According to ar-Razi, most say that God does not change his blessing with punishment unless people turn to evil. But this is not the changing of man's nature. The horse, bear, or elephant may be taught to dance, the tiger to jump through a burning ring of fire. But does this change their nature? You may be very polite and pleasant, but what are you like when you lose your temper?

THE FREEDOM OF THE WILL AND ITS LIMITATIONS

Man is free to choose what he pleases, but since his nature is spoilt by sin, he often chooses according to the demands of his nature. A schoolboy may choose to play and not study. But if he knows that he will suffer for not doing his homework, he will choose to study. For the will to be free, it must be unbiased. Man's nature drives him to choose the wrong, because it is biased towards wrongdoing. He is not compelled to choose the wrong and is responsible for his actions. His state of sin forbids him to choose God without his guidance.

Shaltoot is one of many who state that man has the freedom of choice between good and evil and will be rewarded accordingly.[1] He confuses the issues of man before and after Adam's sin. He pays no heed to the bias of man's nature. As-Sayyed Sabeq makes the same mistake.[2] He quotes: "By the soul and that which shaped it and inspired it to lewdness and godfearing; prosperous is he who purifies it, and failed is he who seduces it" (91:7-10). The verse does not say "to lewdness *or* godfearing," but "to lewdness *and* godfearing." The word "and" links both principles. What the verse teaches is man's responsibility in dealing with what God has given him. The soul that needs purifying cannot be said to be pure. The soul that is seduced falls from goodness.

Another verse is quoted to prove the freedom of the will: "We guided him along the two roads" (90:10). The two roads are good and evil, according to the *Hadith*.[3] Man is born neutral and his parents make him a Jew, a Christian or whatever he may become.[4] The child, when he decides, takes one road or another. But the verse is not ambiguous. It means that God guides man on the road of faith or unbelief, of truth or error. The same can be said of another verse: "We guided him on the way, either thankful or blaspheming" (76:3). It is the response to guidance that is mentioned, not the state of the soul, nor why a man takes one way or another. The truth remains that unless God guides first, none will come to him. Free will, by itself, will not bring a man to God. Freedom means that a man's action is self-determined, even when biased by an evil nature. While Adam's temptation came from without, his progeny's temptation comes from within their own hearts. How greatly do they fall when Satan attacks them!

THE EXAMPLE OF ABRAHAM

We find a practical aspect of guidance in the story of Abraham. Abraham's reason could not allow him to worship his father's idols of stone. Yet he did not know God. He worshipped a planet. When it set, he realized it was not God. So he worshipped the moon, with the same result. Then he said: "If my lord does not guide me, I shall be of the people who are astray" (6:74-83). His Lord did not guide him until after he worshipped the sun.

What made Abraham know God? It was not his intellect, for that did not change from the moment he worshipped the heavenly bodies till the moment he knew God. It was God who guided him and opened his spiritual eyes so that he could see the truth: "And so, we were showing Abraham the kingdom of the heavens and earth so that he might be of those having sure faith" (v.75). Abraham's faith was based on knowledge which he imparted to his father. His father did not receive God's guidance and he remained in his unbelief. Abraham said: "My father, there has come to me a knowledge such as came not to you; follow me and I will guide you on a level path" (19:43).

THE EXAMPLES OF MOSES AND YAHYA (JOHN)

The story of Moses is well known (20:1-46). God chose him when he was a baby, and saved him from death. It was inevitable that he should lead Moses to know him, even after he had killed a man.

Yahya was chosen before he was conceived (3:39). He had to come to a knowledge of God.

God did not foresee, as does a crystal-ball-gazer, that Moses and Yahya would believe in him, and therefore decided to choose them. This would be like someone ordering the sun to rise in the morning, knowing that it will. God's choosing came first, man's followed after. God's will comes before man's will.

It is an insult to God to suggest that he guides those who do good deeds and leads astray those who do evil. As-Sayyed Sabeq makes that mistake.[5] He quotes 13:27 and 29:69 in support of his idea. "He guides to him all who repented." "Those who struggle in our cause, surely we guide them in our ways." What the verses mean is that God continues to guide those who have already known him and repented as a result of his primary guidance. A man cannot repent without guidance, nor will he struggle in God's way without knowing God. As-Sayyed Sabeq gives the glory to man and says that if God guides and leads astray, then there is no freedom of choice to his servants.[6] Man is allowed to choose, but God is denied the freedom. He has to wait till man decides first, then he will follow.

Is man the captain of the ship and God the passenger? Is God's will subservient to man's? What a travesty of the truth. No man can know God unless God initially decides to choose and guide him. Adam did not repent until he was reprimanded. Did God wait for him to speak, or did he address him first? Away with the idea of robbing God of his sovereign will. "God is the light of the heavens and the earth; he guides to his light whomsoever he wills" (24:35). Where is man's action in this verse? There are no conditions for guidance except that God pleases to do so. God is faithful. Once he decides to guide a man, he will see it through, and continue to guide him all his life. Verse 6:82 refers to Abraham and suggests that he was in a continuous state of guidance.

SUMMARY

Sin pollutes the moral character of man, becomes its guiding principle, and produces a feeling of guilt. Mankind has felt this guilt since ancient times, when he sacrificed to appease the gods. Man acts according to his polluted nature which involves his reason, will and desires. He has the freedom of choice in that his actions are self-generated. If you commit adultery, you do it by choice. You have no one to blame but yourself. The universality of sin proves that sin is the driving force in the life of men. The need for forgiveness and God's mercy proves that all men are guilty. God's justice demands that the whole of his law, which is a unit expressing his character, be obeyed. All have failed and come short of God's law. All are under condemnation and the terror of hell. It is necessary for a man's nature to be changed if he is to escape. Yet he must receive the penalty for his guilt which God's law demands. Man is in a dilemma from which he cannot extricate himself. Only God could provide the answer through Jesus Christ. He guides men to his knowledge.

The suggestion that a sinner can desire God by nature is untenable. God must come down and open the way to repentance. His will is the primary mover, and not the follower, of man's will. Once God guides a man, he will continue to do so and will reward obedience with further guidance. But he will also reward disobedience by leading the unbeliever further into error.

Sin produces more sin and unbelief more unbelief. Remember Adam. He had a holy nature and clear instructions from his Lord. If he failed in his state of innocence, who can succeed in his state of sin? If a man comes to know God, it is because of God's great mercy and goodness. The glory belongs to God alone.

References

1. Mahmood Shaltoot, Al-Islam, (Dar ush-Shurooq, Beirut, 1983), p.49.
2. As-Sayyed Sabeq, Al-'aqa-id ul-Islamiyyat, (Beirut, 1985), pp.99-108.

3. Al-Bukhari, vol.6, p.209.
4. Ibid., p.143.
5. As-Sayyed Sabeq, op. cit., p.106.
6. Ibid.

Chapter Thirteen
Civil Government

Nations are organizations of peoples with a culture, faith, language, and government whose arm is the law. Muhammad established a nation which proclaimed one God and himself as his messenger. The nation absorbed believers irrespective of their status in life, or country or tribe of origin. Muhammad was the judge, leader, administrator and chief of the army. He laid down the foundations of a faith which was able to subdue Arabia and the neighbouring countries in Asia, North Africa, and Europe within a few years. Muhammad's political successors, the Khalifahs, extended the conquest after his death.

The nation was established when Muhammad left Makkah for Yathrib (Madinah) in 622 A.D., after twelve years of faithful preaching, when he urged men to forsake their idols and worship the One true God. This began the first year of the Islamic calendar. Muhammad scouted the land from Madinah to determine the intrigue of his enemies. They were the Makkans, of his own tribe of Quraysh, and their Jewish and Arabian allies. The main conflict was to be with Makkah, the leading city of al-Hijaz in culture and trade, situated in the northern region of Arabia. He planned to remove the human barriers in his way. War with Quraysh was inevitable. The migration meant that the phase of peaceful preaching had ended, and the phase of military confrontation had begun. The *Qur'an* came down to meet every situation in the life of the new community. Its verses, together with Muhammad's wisdom, formed the basis of faith and conduct. It was this action of Muhammad, in forming a civil and religious community, that is the basis of the Islamic state. The first Islamic state was a historical development; there were no geographical boundaries within which it was ordained to remain. Its sphere of influence was to be the whole world: "Say, O Mankind, I am the messenger of God to you all; of him to whom belongs the kingdom of the heavens and the earth; there is no God but he" (7:158). The verse was erroneously extended to mean a universal government, rather than a universal message. Muslims must strive to bring the world under the dominion and government of Islam. The kingdom of Christ, by contrast, found its universality in the hearts of believers everywhere.

THE MYTH OF A WORLD GOVERNMENT

History has proved the failure of Islam to establish a world government. Such an objective will never be achieved. Believers in a world government live in a world of fiction, whether they be Muslims, Christians, Socialists, Communists, Traditionalists, Autocrats or Dictators. There are two reasons for this. The first is found in man and the second in God.

The nature of man forbids a unified world government. Very few comprehend the nature of man, because they refuse to accept that the driving force of his nature is sin. How can they govern an unknown entity? They do not even know themselves. Man is quarrelsome, individualistic and selfish. Each individual is the most valuable in his own eyes. Each resents the authority of others and accepts it only where it will work to his benefit.

Is not the history of kingdoms and empires the history of the subjugation by force and the shedding of blood? There is a war in some country of the world at any time, even in countries where faith and culture are identical and where men kill one another in the name of the same God. Intrigue, conspiracy and force are the three weapons used in the struggle for power. They have been the features of every nation, including the Islamic nations. Muslims took arms against one another after Muhammad's death, as they do so today. Who was to determine truth from error? Who fought in the way of God and who against him? This should destroy any argument that it is one's duty to fight for God, when the real truth is a desire to rule over others. Christianity is more reasonable. Although Christ's message is universal (Mt.28:19), it was never intended to achieve world dominion. When organized Christianity aimed to subjugate the nations by force of arms, it did so in contradiction of what its God intended.

The second reason for the impossibility of a world government lies in

God. He will not allow it, for it will lead to the increase of organized sin. Men gathered after the flood to build a city whose tower would reach to heaven (Gen.11:1-9). God confounded their tongue and scattered them in the earth. He divided the people into nations (Deut.32:8). Genesis, Chapter 10, lists the ancient nations of man.

The *Qur'an* acknowledges the futility of a universal nation. "Mankind were only one nation, when they fell into variance" (10:19). "Had your Lord willed, he would have made mankind one nation, but they continued in their differences excepting those on whom the Lord had mercy" (11:118; 16:93). Even those shown mercy were at variance after Muhammad's death. "Had your Lord willed" means he had not willed. Anyone who reads the history of Islam will find that the most striking feature of that history is the struggle for power, when Muslim killed Muslim. Nations and their own prophets will stand as nations, not as one, in judgment before God (7:34; 16:36; 27:83; 28:75; 45:28). We have seen in our day the fragmentation of the Soviet Union, and armed struggle in the nations of the Far and Middle East, in Africa and India. There are groups who would struggle within each nation for further fragmentation and self-rule. Religion is not a safeguard against the selfishness of men. The Iraqi-Iranian war (1980-1988), and the invasion of Kuwait by Iraq in August 1990 are proof of this. If it is argued that men do not obey God when they initiate such wars, I say, this is precisely my argument.

RELIGION AND SECULAR LIFE

Muslims claim that the *Qur'an* is unique in establishing an inseparable link between faith and the order of life. The protagonists of such an idea failed to study the history of the children of Israel in the *Old Testament*.

No religion can be called a religion if it does not expect its followers to adhere to its teachings and customs. This is particularly true of the heavenly religions. When God made a covenant with the people in the days of Moses, they said: "All the words which the Lord has said, we will do" (Ex.19:8; 24:3,4). A form of government was laid down for them. Every movement in life was governed by God's law. Religion and life were one. Life was religion. History shows how they failed to live under the rule of God, and how they rejected his government.

The government of most lands is based upon religion and the beliefs of its rulers. Christian principles are reflected in the legal system of the lands where Christianity predominates, Islamic principles in Islamic lands, and Buddhist principles in Buddhist lands.

Religious men tend towards fanaticism and tyranny. They think that they have the authority of God to support them, and become less merciful than unbelieving rulers. Where freedom of faith is lost, men are governed by tyrants. Men of religion are intolerant of dissenting views and become the destroyers of freedom. Their nations are shackled by chains too strong for them to remove.

THE ALLEGED QUR'ANIC BASIS FOR AN ISLAMIC STATE

The *Qur'an* calls for obedience to God and Muhammad, not for the setting up of a universal Islamic government. "O Believers, obey God and obey the messenger and those in authority among you, and should you quarrel in anything refer it to God and the messenger" (4:59). The verse is said to lay down three principles: obedience to God; obedience to Muhammad; and obedience to those in authority in an Islamic administration. It is supported by 7:3 and, by deduction, 5:51,57, which call for a rejection of the authority of non-believers.

The verses do not call for the setting up of a state, but for obedience to God and to those in charge in the community. The word "awliya," which is translated to mean "those in authority," also means "friends." Historically, they were the leaders of the military raids of the time. The Qur'anic evidence for a universal Islamic state is indeed scanty. The precedence of Muhammad remains the only true reason for the assertion.

The occasion for the giving of 4:59 is interesting.[1] It was a private dispute between two men, and has no relationship to civil government. The occasion showed the bigotry and conflict between two close friends of Muhammad. Khalid ibn el-Waleed headed a raid upon an Arab settlement. 'Ammar bin Yaser went with him. They determined to attack the following morning. The Arabs fled except for one man who declared his Islam to 'Ammar. 'Ammar promised him security of life and possessions. When they entered the settlement, none was found apart from the man. Khalid imprisoned him and confiscated his goods. 'Ammar protested saying that the man had declared his Islam. Khalid was angry with 'Ammar for promising the man peace without his permission. Feelings ran high, and they resorted to Muhammad's judgment. They cursed each other in his presence. Khalid called 'Ammar a slave. Muhammad justly ruled in favour of 'Ammar and said that whoever curses 'Ammar God curses him. Khalid repented and they made their peace. The verse then came, saying, "If you quarrel on anything, refer it to God and the messenger." Khalid may have been the sword of God, but he was bigoted and proud. Other tales tell of a quarrel between individuals. How can one conclude that the occasion of a personal conflict has anything to do with the matter of government? If men cursed each other in Muhammad's presence, how do you expect them to behave when he was no longer there?

THE STORY OF JOSEPH

Joseph's story is used by some to prove that only an Islamic government is legal, and that a non-Muslim may not share in an Islamic government: "So we established Joseph in the land to make his dwelling wherever he would." He said: "O my Lord, you have given me rule" (12:56,101). Such verses are used to surmise that Joseph established an Islamic government in Egypt![2] A theory is proved by accepting it as a fact and using it to prove itself. It is said that Joseph would not have accepted to rule with a heathen king; therefore he established an Islamic state. It is like saying "A dog is a dog because it is a dog." Neither the *Qur'an* nor the *Bible* nor archaeological evidence shows that an Islamic state was in existence at the time of the Pharaohs. Verse 12:54 says: "Today you are firmly established in our favour." Who shows favour upon another? Is it not the ruler, upon his subjects? Pharaoh said: "Only in the throne will I be greater than you" (Gen.41:40). The priesthood remained in Egypt. Joseph could not take the land of the priests from them, because Pharaoh reserved them their portion of bread (Gen.47:22). Did Joseph govern by the yet unknown Islamic Shari'ah?

Another verse is abused to justify a false idea: "Say, my Lord, lead me with a just ingoing and lead me with a just outgoing; grant me authority for you, to help me" (17:80). Muhammad was asked to pray this prayer when he went to Madinah from the enmity of Quraysh. It is a request for God to strengthen his hand and grant him the authority to spread his message and vanquish his enemies. It is a prayer for the consolidation of strength in the use of force.

THE RULE OF GOD OR HIS DEFEAT?

The fact that God is the ruler of the heavens and earth does not mean that he ordained the Shari'ah to be the legal necessity for mankind. "You give the kingdom to whom you will and seize it from whom you will" (3:26) is said to mean that God was to give Muhammad the Persian and Byzantine empires. Verses 2:107 and 5:17,120 give the rule to God and whomsoever he wills. Many other verses ascribe the kingdom to God without reference to Muhammad (2:247; 40:29). It is a basic message of the *Qur'an* that God the king, does what pleases him, and can replace one creation by another (14:19; 4:133).

The argument for Islam goes like this. God is ruler over all. Muhammad was his messenger to mankind. What God and Muhammad said became the order of life to all men. "Religion with God is Islam" (3:19). "Whosoever desires other than Islam as religion, it will not be accepted of him" (3:85). Non-Islamic governments are therefore illegitimate. The whole world must come under the authority of Islam.

The conclusion which Muslims have drawn from these verses is false. The universal message of Islam is taught, not its necessity to subjugate the world. The argument makes mockery of God, because he becomes a helpless observer, unable to wrench the rule from the non-Islamic governments of the world. He is a figurehead. Men usurp authority and he just looks helplessly on. If God divides people into nations, giving power to whom he wills and removing whomever he wills, then the President of the United States of America and the last General Secretary of the Soviet Union, and every ruler on earth, have been placed there by his authority. If they are not, then God is defeated in his purpose. He cannot execute his will. The world is full of illegitimate governments and he can do nothing about it. He rules only in name. Such are the implications of al-Mawdudi's argument.[3] It is useless making God as helpless as idols of wood and stone.

Should Muslims usurp authority in a non-Islamic land to bring about the rule of God? Should they not aim to convert the land to Islam, then rule legitimately? Why did Muhammad send his early followers to the Christian land of Ethiopia for fear of the persecution of Quraysh? The ruler an-Najashi refused to hand them over to 'Amr ibn el-'As, who was yet unconverted to Islam. Muslims like to think that an-Najashi adopted Islam. This is not true. He assented to the *Qur'an*'s description of Jesus as the word of God, but did not revoke his faith in his divinity.

"O People, we created you from male and female and made you nations and tribes to know each other, surely the most honourable of you with God is the most devout" (49:13). He "has made of one blood all nations of men to dwell on the earth, and has determined the times before appointed, and the bounds of their habitation" (Acts 17:26). Nations exist according to their appointed time. They come and go and others take their place (10:49). Akkad, Babylon, Assyria, Chaldea, Greece, Persia, Rome, Byzantium, and even the great Arab, Turkish and British empires came and went. If God is not in control of the nations and their rulers, then he is not in control of anything. He is a defeated God.

CONFLICT FOR POWER OR THE DEATH OF RELIGION

Before Muhammad died in June 632 A.D., he captured Makkah. The Arabian tribes of the peninsula entered Islam. The tribes turned back from Islam after his death, and were returned by Abu Bakr, the first Khalifah, through the sword of Khalid ibn el-Waleed. It was a political necessity. The tribes were needed for the Islamic conquests beyond Arabia. The main object of this section is to show that in conflict for power among the Muslims, Islam did not differ in the least from the patterns of the nations of the world. As Sennecharib was killed by his sons and Esarhaddon reigned in his place, and as one Roman Emperor killed his predecessor, so the Muslims fought it out, while ordinary men did their battles for them. Religion is primarily for the eternal welfare of men. What does it matter who rules, as long as justice and equity cover the land? When the affairs of this world become paramount, religion is thrown into the abyss. Islam fell into the same trap as the Jewish people who rejected their God's rule. Theirs was a theocracy, in which God governed them by his law through his chosen prophets and judges. Islam is a theocracy also, where God governs through the successors or Khalifahs of Muhammad by means of the Islamic law or Shari'ah. As the Jewish theocracy failed, so did the Islamic. Some modern Islamic nations are rife with injustice. Men's minds and mouths are tightly shut, lest they think or speak what does not please those in authority over them.

'Uthman bin 'Affan, the third Khalifah, was murdered in 656. The reciters of the *Qur'an* stood against him, because he destroyed their copies when he gathered one *Qur'an*. They could no longer prove the truth of their recitations, which differed from the *Qur'an* of today. He also appropriated the spoils of war for himself, his family, and the business of the state. 'Aisha, Muhammad's wife, was against him. With his murder began a period of struggle in Islam which characterized its history. 'Ali bin abi Taleb, Muhammad's cousin, reluctantly accepted the Khalifate. He was a staunch supporter of 'Uthman. 'Ali was challenged by Talhah, and az-Zubayr 'Aisha's nephew, and their followers in al-Iraq and al-Hijaz. 'Ali was the first to accept Muhammad's message. He was a true Muslim worthy of the Khalifate. The conflict was for power and not religion. 'Ali won the battle of the Camel near Basrah in December 656.[4] Imagine Muhammad's wife fighting his cousin, who was husband to his daughter!

Mu'awiyah, son of Abu Sufyan (the one time arch-enemy of Muhammad), was governor of Syria. He demanded that 'Ali bring 'Uthman's murderers to justice or resign the Khalifate.⁵ The Syrian army of Mu'awiyah met the Iraqi army of 'Ali at Siffin, on the bank of the Euphrates, in the thirty-seventh year of the Hijra. At-Tabari describes the fighting and severe enmity between the two camps, and the deception against 'Ali.⁶ 'Ali was about to win the battle when 'Amr ibn el-'As, Mu'awiyah's general who conquered Egypt in the days of 'Umar, made his men raise leaves of the *Qur'an* upon their lances.⁷ This was a call for negotiation based upon the *Qur'an*. They agreed that the representative of each should renounce his allegiance to his master, and that a new Khalifah will be chosen. When 'Ali's representative renounced 'Ali, 'Amr chose Mu'awiyah rather than renounce him.⁸,⁹ He tricked 'Ali, who was later killed by the Kharjites who refused arbitration.¹⁰ Mu'awiyah's Khalifate was established in 659, when the memory of Muhammad was still fresh in the minds of men.

The supporters of 'Ali, the fathers of the Shi'ites, refused Mu'awiyah's Umayyad succession. 'Ali's eldest son, al-Hasan, was appointed in Iraq as the legitimate Khalifah. Some of his supporters in the Persian capital went over to Mu'awiyah, until al-Hasan made peace with Mu'awiyah.¹¹ He died in 669, probably of poisoning. Mu'awiyah placed his son Yazid as Khalifah after him. Thus the Khalifate became hereditary, like the kingships of the nations. 'Ali's other son, al-Husayn, refused to accept Yazid. He was met in battle at Karbala' by the governor of al-Kufah on behalf of Yazid and was killed. His head was sent to Yazid in Damascus.¹²,¹³ That was the fate of 'Ali's sons, Muhammad's grandsons from Fatimah, Muhammad's daughter.

DESTRUCTION OF THE KA'BAH

'Abdullah, son of az-Zubayr, became ruler in Makkah and Madinah after al-Husayn's death. He was supported by the Ansar, Muhammad's one-time supporters of the Aws and Khazraj tribes. The men of al-Hiajz joined him. Yazid's troops defeated him in battle east of Madinah. He fled and took refuge in the holy mosque. The mosque was bombarded with catapults by the general of the invading army. During the siege, the Ka'bah was destroyed and the Black Stone split into three pieces.¹⁴ The siege was lifted in 683. Abraha the Ethiopian moved against the Ka'bah in 570, the year Muhammad was born. God saved his house, according to the *Qur'an* (105:1-5). But just fifty years after Muhammad's death, the Ka'bah was burnt and the Black Stone fractured and the holy mosque attacked in the war of Muslim against Muslim. 'Abdullah established himself in al-Hijaz and placed his brother over Iraq. He himself ruled over the south of Arabia, Egypt and part of Syria. He was eventually destroyed by al-Hajjaj ibn Yusuf ath-Thaqafi in the seventy-third year of the Hijra.[15,16] His head was taken to Damascus. The power of the Ansar was broken forever. Al-Hajjaj was said to have killed 10,000 men in his life time. He extended Umayyad authority into Asia.

One further episode is worth mentioning. It is the massacre of the Umayyad house by the 'Abbasid general 'Abdullah, the butcher, in 750 A.D.[17] The Umayyads were invited to a banquet and butchered. Eighty were murdered and the rest hunted. 'Abd er-Rahman escaped to Spain where he established Umayyad rule. There were, at one time, three concurrent Khalifates: the Umayyad in Spain (929-1031), the 'Abbasid in Baghdad (750-1258), and the Fatimid in Cairo (909-1171).

The histories of at-Tabari, ibn Atheer and ibn Khaldoon detail Islamic history, and often day-to-day events. The history is filled with slaughter, often of the best in the land. The *Qur'an* forbade Muslims from killing one another and promised hell for such a deed. It asked them to make peace between two conflicting parties (49:9,10). It foresaw what would happen. Who was right and who was wrong, since the warring parties all claimed God's support? Who would be in the garden and who in hell? It is a sobering thought. Is a unified Islamic government possible? I think not. The Arab will refuse to have a Pakistani rule over him in his land. The Pakistani will refuse the authority of an Afghani in his land. The state is no longer concerned with spiritual welfare of men, but with political expediency and power. Religion perishes in the process.

THE PLIGHT OF THE JEWISH PEOPLE UNDER THE LAW OF GOD

The study of the history of the children of Israel gives us another angle upon the matter of the religious state. Theirs was a typical example of the marriage of life and religion. Religion was inseparable from life to a greater extent than is found in Islam. Muslims failed to learn from their example. The Jew's bondage to the law was planned by God to show men, in a practical way, the impossibility of living by his law. The need for a saviour was inevitable.

The law of God, given through Moses, could be divided into five parts of a unified whole. The law of Worship demanded the worship of God alone. The Moral Law is embodied in the Ten and other Commandments (Ex.21-23; Lev.17-23). The Ceremonial law was concerned with washings and physical cleanliness from pollution (Lev.12,15,22; Num.19). It included permitted and forbidden food and various religious feasts. The Sacrificial law laid down the circumstances and means of sacrifice and its necessity (Lev.1-6). Sacrifice was to be offered daily by the priests on behalf of the nation and individuals. The Judicial law was scattered in the *Torah*, and laid down the punishments for sin and for failure to keep the other parts of the law. Death was prescribed for several sins.

Men and women had to be careful what to touch, what to eat, what to say, and how to behave in every detail of life. They were routinely washing ceremonially, offering sacrifices and observing feasts and communal gatherings. If you were to read the *Torah*, commencing from the latter half of the book of Exodus through Leviticus and Numbers, you would find most of the law there. It was extensive, binding, and rigid. It robbed men of their liberty. They were the servants of God and were not free to disobey. They agreed to keep his covenant through obedience to his law. The law was an irksome burden they could not carry. The rest of the *Old Testament* is the story of their disobedience and punishment, their exile and captivity. The book of Acts tells of an event in the history of the early church when certain men wanted the non-Jewish believers to observe the law of Moses. Peter said that God "put no difference between us and them, purifying their hearts by faith. Now therefore, why tempt God, to put a yoke upon the neck of the disciples, which neither our fathers nor we were able to carry?" (Acts 15:5-10).

REJECTION OF GOD'S RULE

During the era before Christ, God governed his people through a theocracy. He was their king. He raised up judges to deliver the people from their enemies and to judge between them. He sent them prophets for special occasions, especially when they departed from his ways. After they were in Canaan for some years, they desired a king to rule over them and to go before them in battle. It was not God's intention, but they insisted. God gave them their desire in the days of Samuel. He said: "Hear the voice of the people in all that they say to you, for they have not rejected you, but they have rejected me, that I should rule over them" (1Sam.8:7). God chose Saul, then David, then Solomon, then his successor. The kingship later descended from father to son.

COMPARISON BETWEEN THE JEWISH KINGDOM AND THE KHALIFATE

Personal Conflict for Power

When God rejected Saul for his disobedience and chose David in his stead, Saul sought the life of David. He wanted to frustrate God's plan, though he knew that God had chosen David. Muslims gathered armies to fight Muslims in the struggle of their respective leaders for the Khalifate.

Inheritance of Power

As the Khalifate came down from father to son, so did the kingdom of Israel 1650 years earlier.

Conspiracy

The conspiracy was such that David's son Absalom rose against him to snatch the kingdom. This caused a division of the nation into two camps. The books of Kings and Chronicles detail how the kingdom was usurped by servants and generals alike. Kings were slain in the process. The story of the Khalifate mirrors this.

Division of the Kingdom

After Solomon's death, the kingdom was divided into the northern kingdom of Israel and the southern kingdom of Judah. There were like divisions in Islam into Sunnis, Shi'ites and others, whose differences produced enmity. There were three Khalifates at one time, engendered by wars and disagreement. The Jewish kingdoms fought each other, and allied themselves—with Egyptians, Syrians, or Assyrians—against their brothers as policy demanded.

The Demise of Religion by the Hands of the Rulers

This took place as God called his people back. Many kings did evil, and encouraged idolatry and Baal worship. Those who opposed them were persecuted. Al-Hajjaj provides a similar example in Islam. He worshipped God, and cut the necks of his opponents. Religion had a superficial role in the hearts of rulers who dared to kill their fellow Muslims in order to maintain their authority over the nation.

Brother Killed Brother in the Faith

There was no difference between the wars of the Jewish tribes and the Muslims' wars in the struggle for power.

THE IMPLICATION OF THE GOSPEL IN WARFARE

"God has bought from believers themselves and their possessions, because to them belongs the garden: they fight in the way of God; they kill and are killed; that is the promise binding upon him in the *Torah* and the *Gospel* and the *Qur'an*" (9:111).

The *Torah* tells of the conquest of Canaan by the command of God, and also of the punishment of idolaters by the hand of their fellows (Ex.32:26-28; 1Ki.18). There is no such command in the *Gospel* of peace. The Christian's warfare is spiritual, not carnal (2Cor.10:4; 1Tim.6:12). "Put on the whole armour of God that you may be able to stand against the wiles of the devil, for we wrestle not against flesh and blood, but against principalities and powers, against the rulers of the darkness of the world, against spiritual wickedness in high places" (Eph.6:11,12). The fight is against the devil, not men. The *Gospel* never calls for the shedding of the blood of another in order to spread the faith or preserve it. The Christians of the first three centuries suffered extreme persecution without raising a sword or spear in their own defence. Jesus asked men to follow him and establish his kingdom on earth in the heart.

Al-Mawdudi misinterpreted the *Gospels* to prove that Jesus called his followers to kill in his name.[18] "Blessed are they who are persecuted for righteousness' sake, for theirs is the kingdom of heaven" (Mt.5:10). Jesus did not say, "Blessed are they who kill for righteousness' sake, for theirs is the kingdom of earth." Those who are persecuted are those who suffer for their faith, like Bilal did, and Muhammad and his followers at the hands of Quraysh. Al-Mawdudi quoted further: "He that finds his life shall lose it, and he that loses his life for my sake shall find it" (Mt.10:39). "Everyone that has forsaken houses, or brothers, or sisters, or father, or mother, or wife, or children, or lands for my name's sake, shall inherit everlasting life" (Mt.19:29). Where is the command to fight? The followers of Christ suffered at the hands of others: "All that will live godly in Christ Jesus shall suffer persecution" (2Tim.3:12). Al-Mawdudi put the victims in place of their oppressors.

Christ taught his disciples to live a peaceable life. "Resist not evil, but whoever shall smite you on your right cheek, turn to him the other also, and if a man will sue you at the law and take away your coat, let him have your cloak also; and whosoever shall compel you to go a mile, go with him two." (Mt.5:39-41). "Love your enemies, bless them that curse you, do good to them that hate you, and pray for them who despitefully use you and persecute you" (Mt.5:44). Such is the Christians's code of conduct in his everyday life.

When Jesus stood before Pilate, he said to him: "My kingdom is not of this world: if my kingdom were of this world, then would my servants fight" (Jn.18:36). When one of his disciples tried to defend him at his arrest, he said to him: "Put up your sword into its place: for they that take by the sword shall perish with the sword" (Mt.26:52). When he was crucified he prayed for forgiveness upon those who did the deed (Lk.23:34). When Jesus, according to the *Qur'an*, said, "Fear God and obey me" (3:50), he did not mean kill for God's sake. He said to his disciples: "A new commandment I give to you, that you love one another as I have loved you, even so love one another" (Jn.13:34). It is a gross misinterpretation of the *Gospel* to stain it with the blood of unbelievers. Christianity grew by the blood of its own people, slain by others.

THE EARTHLY KINGSHIP OF CHRIST

The prophets of Israel said: "Behold your king comes to you, he is just, and having salvation; lowly and riding upon an ass and upon a colt, the foal of an ass" (Zech.9:9). The four *Gospel* accounts report how Jesus entered Jerusalem as king, one week before his crucifixion, not riding a stallion but the colt of an ass (Mt.21:1-9; Mk.11:1-10; Lk.19:29-38; Jn.12:12-15). The maximum honour he received was the inscription above his cross: "Jesus of Nazareth, the king of the Jews" (Mt.27:37; Mk.15:26; Lk.23:38; Jn19:19). It was written in Greek, Latin and Hebrew, the main languages of the world then, as a signal to all mankind. Pilate refused to alter the statement at the request of the Jews (Jn.19:21,22). The fact, by God's provision, had to be made known to all. The crown which Jesus wore was a crown of thorns, his sceptre the nails in his hands, his throne the cross. His true kingship is in the hearts of those who believe in his name. He reigns supreme.

GOVERNMENT ACCORDING TO THE NEW TESTAMENT

Jesus did not intend to establish a Christian government. When a man said to him, "Master, speak to my brother that he divide the inheritance with me," he answered, "Man, who made me a judge and a divider over you?" (Lk.12:13,14). When he was asked whether tax should be paid, he said: "Render unto Caesar the things that are Caesar's, and unto God the things that are God's" (Mt.22:21). In other words, let Caesar rule his domain, and let him not interfere in the things of God. Jesus was not a revolutionary. He paid his taxes. This is far removed from what the Christian Church did when it gained respectability and power, so that the pope was stronger than the king. Oppression and injustice ruled, due to the departure of men from the simple teaching of their Lord.

The *Qur'an* says: "God gives the kingdom to whomsoever he wills and seizes it from whomsoever he wills." (3:26). This is what the *Bible* teaches (Dan.2:21,37; 4:17,25). Jesus said to Pilate: "You could have no power over me, except it were given you from above" (Jn.19:11). His disciples taught the same thing. Paul said in a letter to the Roman Christians: "Let every soul be subject to the higher powers, for there is no power but of God: the powers that be are ordained of God. Whosoever therefore resists the power, resists the ordinance of God: and they that resist shall receive to themselves damnation, for rulers are not a terror to good works, but to evil." "Render therefore to all their dues: tribute to whom tribute; custom to whom custom; fear to whom fear; honour to whom honour" (Ro.13:1-7). Peter said the same thing: "Submit yourselves to every ordinance of man for the Lord's sake: whether it be for the king as supreme, or to governors as to them that are sent by him for the punishment of evildoers, and for the praise of them that do well;" "as free, and not using your liberty for a cloak of maliciousness, but as servants of God. Honour all men, love the brotherhood, fear God, honour the king" (1Pet.2:13-17). A Christian believer must abide by the law and work for the good of his fellow citizens. He must honour those in authority and speak no evil of them. When he is in an Islamic land, he should respect the rulers even more than his Muslim friends do.

THE ROLE OF THE CHURCH IN CIVIL AND SOCIAL AFFAIRS

Since laws are enacted by governments, it is desirable for a Christian to attain to a position of authority, to affect the passing of just laws. It is not the function of the organized church to do this. The church should be involved in the social welfare of society, but not in politics. It may not support one political party against another. Alienation of sections of society, even within the Christian community, will ensue. Christians influence society for good. William Wilberforce was responsible for the abolition of the slave trade through a bill in Parliament in 1807. The historian A. J. Grant stated the reason that revolution did not take place in England in the eighteenth century, when wars raged in Europe: "The wide influence of Wesleyanism was a force that made the spread of revolutionary ideas impossible, in just those classes that were most revolutionary in France".[20] A revival of Biblical Christianity took place through John Wesley (1703-1791).

Christians have always been the conscience of society. They have built hospitals and nursing homes, and cared for the elderly, sick and infirm, the hungry and naked in all nations of the world. This is why many Christians take up medicine and nursing. The primary duty of the church as a body lies in the spiritual sphere. It should not ignore the bodies of men, nor fail to cry out against tyranny, oppression and injustice. Confusion should be avoided between what Christ taught, and the evil that men do in his name. Muslims tend to think that so-called Christian countries follow the standard of Christ. This is far from the truth, just as Islamic countries do not follow the teaching of the *Qur'an*. More oppression was done by supposed Christians, and a church gone astray from true religion, than one cares to mention. Men appropriate to themselves what God prohibits. God is not responsible for their evil deeds. Religion is equal to politics in producing fanaticism and injustice. Any group of men may magnify a certain aspect of life and become tyrants. Religious men are not immune, but have a propensity to do just that. They may have a cause, but so does every dictator, even if his cause is to claim another's land as his own. Such was the case with conquerors such as Nebuchadnezzar, Alexander, Julius Caesar, Genghis Khan, Napoleon Bonaparte and Hitler.

SUMMARY

This chapter intends to show that it is futile for a religious system of government to control the world. If man forms one organized government, there will be no limit to the evil he is capable of doing. If a government is religious in content, there will be no limit to tyranny and oppression. Islam used the same means as other nations in its struggle for power, and Muslim killed Muslim at the whim of rulers. It even spread through war, and not by peaceful preaching of its message. The direct rule of the law of God upon men will cause their destruction. God's standard is too severe and demanding. He will not allow the smallest offence to go unpunished. Theocracy failed in the case of the children of Israel. God was setting a practical example for men, of the fact that they cannot abide by his austere law which controls what a man should touch or think. His object was not to show men that they are better off without him, but that they need his grace and salvation to deliver them from the sin which is found in their nature. Islam failed to learn from the Jewish example. It aims to control the world politically, against the teaching of the *Qur'an*, which said that God divided men into nations, and gives the rule to whom he pleases.

References

1. Al-Wahidi, Asbab nuzool el-Qur'an (Jeddah, 1984), p.152.
2. Abu el-'Ala' el-Mawdudi. Al-hukoomat el-Islamiyyat, (Ad-Dar

us-Su'audiyyat, Jeddah, 1984), pp.52-56.
3. Ibid.,p.74.
4. Abu Ja'far Muhammad bin Jareer et-Tabari, Tareekh ul-Umam wal-Mulook, (Dar Swaidan, Beirut), vol.4, pp.508-548.
5. Ibid., vol. 5, 5-9.
6. Ibid., pp.5-48
7. Ibid., pp.48-63.
8. Ibid., pp.67-71.
9. Philip K. Hitti, History of the Arabs, (The Macmillan Press Ltd., London, 1970), p.181.
10. At-Tabari, vol.5. pp.64-66,72.
11. Ibid., pp.400-467.
12. Ibid.
13. Hitti, Op. Cit., p.190.
14. Ibid., p.193.
15. At-Tabari, vol.6, pp.174,175,187-193.
16. Hitti, Op. Cit., pp.191-193.
17. As-Suyuti, Tareekh ul-Khulafa', (Dar ul-Qalam, Beirut, 1986), p.295.
18. Hitti, Op. Cit., p.285.
19. Al-Mawdudi, Op. Cit., p.110.
20. A.J.Grant, Europe, The Last Five Centuries, (Longmans, Green and Co., London. 1955), p.710.

Chapter Fourteen
Liberty

The most amazing fact of human history is the murder done in God's name. There was a time when the church was the official torturer and executioner of those whom it regarded as infidels—men and women who disagreed with some point of its teaching. If cultural differences are the main reason for conflict, it remains a fact that cultures are a product of different religious, moral and secular views.

The function of religion is twofold: to prepare men for their eternal destiny, and to safeguard the quality of life upon earth.

The eternal function is the more important. Man's life is short and full of trouble. His eternal destiny is a permanent state, where time has no presence. If a man is killed for reasons which concern his eternal destiny, he loses forever the chance of mending his ways. It follows that the killer has no real interest in the eternity of another, and therefore no real interest in the main function of religion. The reasonable method would be to convince others by persuasion: "Argue with them in that which is better" (16:125), says the *Qur'an*.

The social reason is also important. It is the right of man to live without hunger, nakedness and the like. Human relationships produce injustice. Religion should strive for justice between men.

LIBERTY OF CONSCIENCE IS A BASIC HUMAN RIGHT

Liberty does not mean a licence to do what one pleases. Due regard must be given to the rights and customs of others. One should not have the liberty of going naked in the streets, unless the culture of the tribe permits nakedness. Robbery and theft are wrong in any society. We can differentiate between two kinds of liberty: that which is bound by custom, and that which is bound by the principles of basic communal life. Murder and adultery fall into the latter category. To indulge in them is to rob a man of his life or his wife.

It is a basic tenet of life that man is free to choose his destiny. Islam emphasizes that God creates men with a free will. Christianity teaches that the will is corrupted. The liberty to choose one's faith falls in the realm of conscience. No man has a claim upon another man's conscience. To rob a man of the liberty to believe according to his conscience is to deny him his God-given liberty. It is equal to robbing God of his gifts to men. This is worse than robbing a man of his wife or goods: it is like robbing him of his very soul. The conscience is strictly private property, and must not be subjected to the will of others. If the conscience is subjugated, a state of tyranny exists. Men have been sent to the gallows, or shot, or sent to psychiatric clinics, or "brainwashed" and reduced to the state of animals for conscience' sake. Death is often preferable than the loss of the freedom of the conscience. No man has the right to be the robber of another's conscience.

RELIGIOUS FANATICISM: A ROBBER OF THE CONSCIENCE

Historically, both Islam and Christianity acted as the robbers of men's conscience when they denied them the freedom to believe or not to believe. They acted contrary to their books. The one notable exception was the case of the children of Israel, who were forbidden to depart from God. Their case was a historical parable. God sought to teach mankind that they need a saviour, in that they cannot meet the demands of his law in worship and deeds of holiness. Christians are the willing servants or slaves of Jesus Christ. Their liberty is to serve him out of love and not coercion. If they fall away, he will deal with them. God has not given men to be the judges of the conscience of other men.

There is a tremendous difference between the Christian and the Islamic concepts. If a man will not be a willing slave of God, let him not be a slave at all. In the Makkan days of Islam, men chose the service of God and suffered in his service. They deemed his obedience more precious than their lives. Faith was adopted out of personal liberty. When Islam entered its militant phase, many adopted the faith out of fear. They lost their liberty. Anyone who fears to believe according to his conscience is in bondage. Those who willingly adopt a religion or a philosophy or a political system without conviction, must be labelled as hypocrites.

LIBERTY OF SPEECH

I use the case of blasphemy as an extreme example. It was punishable by death under the law of Moses (Lev.24:11-14). Blasphemy was not only through words. Deeds of idolatry and disobedience were regarded as blasphemous. If it is argued that blasphemy must be removed from the land, lest the feeble minded be influenced by bad example, then every evil must also be removed. The Muslims did not turn back from their faith when they heard their enemies blaspheme. Blasphemy is offensive to God and man. It flouts the principles of decency. I do not defend the ignorant and arrogant who set themselves against God. He will judge them in due course. If the law of blasphemy on the statute books of the United Kingdom is applied, many will be found guilty, including prominent men in the church. The name of Christ is daily blasphemed and used as a swear-word in every walk of life. Some bishops and ministers of the Gospel regard him as the illegitimate son of Mary. Others say he was a homosexual. Can you imagine such obscenities? Should one take a gun and shoot such corrupters of other men's minds? Christ is not helpless to defend his name: "By your words you shall be justified, and by your words you shall be condemned" (Mt. 12:37). Words are a mirror of the heart. A blasphemer is not a believer in God. Should all unbelievers be killed, or only those who declare their unbelief by means of filthy words? The apostle Paul was a staunch Jew who persecuted Christians and forced some to blaspheme. Christ met him on the way to Damascus and told him that he was persecuting him. This led to Paul's conversion. He became a great preacher of the Gospel until he was beheaded for Christ's sake in Rome. Many of the staunch supporters of Muhammad were blasphemers at the start.

If religion cannot stand up to criticism, argument and bad words, it betrays a fundamental deficiency. Violence becomes a shield against public scrutiny. The Christian does not fear for his faith. Christ said that the gates of hell will not prevail against his Church (Mt.16:18).

The *Gospel* declares the divinity of Christ and the Holy Spirit and denies salvation other than by the name of Christ (Acts 4:12). The *Qur'an* says: "They have blasphemed who said that God is the Christ, the son of Mary" (5:17,72). It even denies the death of Christ. It removes the very heart of the *Gospel*. It is ridiculous to suggest that Christians and Muslims should fight it out until one group exterminates the other.

LIBERTY OF FAITH

During the life of Muhammad, all that was necessary for a man to enter Islam was to confess belief in the One God and in Muhammad as his messenger. The Christian equivalent is contained in the words: "If you shall confess with your mouth the Lord Jesus and shall believe in your heart that God raised him from the dead, you shall be saved" (Ro.10:9). True faith is proved by good works. Hypocrisy is shunned in both the *Qur'an* and the *Bible*. It is only God who knows the heart. A man may appear to be good to his closest friends, but may harbour in his heart thoughts of hatred and adultery. God is not deceived. A man who builds his life on selfishness and greed and lust is neither a Muslim nor a Christian, despite his confession of faith. It is God who knows the soul, not man. There is, however, a measure of honesty in so-called Christian lands which is not known in Islamic lands. A man may reject God openly and not be harmed in Christian societies. In Islamic communities, a man would fear for his life if he were to reject Islam and adopt another faith. It is easier for him not to believe at all. Men are prisoners of society. Men and women do what is expected of them. They have to accept the dogmas without recourse to conscience. This is tyranny indeed.

THE CASE OF UNBELIEVERS

Fighting unbelievers was to be retaliatory: "Slay them wherever you come upon them and expel them from where they expelled you, and trial is more grievous than slaying" (2:190,191). Trial, according to ar-Razi, included persecution and torture. He quoted 'Abdullah bin Jahsh who wrote to the believers in Makkah after the verse came down: "If they shame you for fighting in the holy month, shame them for their unbelief." Unbelievers drove the Muslims out of their homes and threatened their lives. The response was to fight in retaliation, not in aggression. The trial or persecution agrees with the context. The *Hadith* mentions a conversation between 'Umar's son and another man. 'Umar's son said that they fought unbelievers in Muhammad's time when Muslims were few and were persecuted and bound. But when Muslims became many, there was no persecution.[1] He implied that there was no need for retaliation. The modern meaning of the Arabic word "fitnat," translated as "trial," means "conspiracy." Treachery is among the ugliest of crimes known to man.

BE NOT AGGRESSORS

"Fight in the way of God those who fight you and do not aggress, for God does not love the aggressors" (2:190; 5:87).

This verse lays down a principle based upon the character of God, which makes it immutable, unchanging, permanent, not given to abrogation or recission. God says, be merciful for I am merciful, do no evil for I hate evil, be not aggressors for I do not love aggressors. The verse calls for defensive fighting: fight those who fight you. The Arabic word for "fight," means "kill" or cause to die." It is clear that the verse deals with physical warfare and combat, not fighting with words or ideas. This, together with the prohibition of aggression, means fight physically those who fight you physically, but be not the starters of a fight.

The historical background concerns the Makkans before the conquest of Makkah. Muhammad agreed with them that he and his men should have the freedom to roam around the Ka'bah for three days. He feared their treachery, and being wise, warned his men to be ready for a fight if the Makkans broke their covenant of peace. Had he left the matter at that, the verse could be understood to apply only to its historical setting. Having added, "God does not love the aggressor," he placed the matter on a different, more permanent level. The soundness of this exposition is seen in verse 191, which calls the believers to fight them where the others chose to fight the believers, meaning retaliation. Verse 192 closes the argument by saying: "But if they desist, then God is forgiving and merciful," that is, stop fighting if they stop.

Some mistakenly think that the non-aggression command refers to not fighting women and children. This is stated by most commentators. It is not true, and makes nonsense of the verse, which specifically refers to fighting in a retaliatory manner. The alleged referral to women and children is an attempt to get out of an interpretation which appears to make the *Qur'an* contradict itself. The truth is that Muslims have misinterpreted the whole issue of fighting. They have aggressed in their conquests of lands beyond Arabia. Muslim historians have established this fact beyond doubt. There is no reconciliation between the command to fight in the way of God and that prohibiting aggression. The prohibitive command is final, being based upon the unchanging attributes of God.

THE PEOPLE OF THE BOOK

"O Believers, the idolaters are indeed filthy; so let them not come near to the holy mosque after this year of theirs. If you fear poverty, God shall surely enrich you of his bounty, if he will. God is knowing, wise. Fight those who believe not in God and the last day and do not forbid what God and his messenger have forbidden, such men as practice not the religion of truth, being those who have been given the Book, until they pay tribute out of hand, being humiliated" (9:28,29).

The first verse forbade idolaters the holy mosque where trade was carried out in the vicinity. The poverty of the believers was to be eased by the tribute from the Jews and Christians, who were to be spared if they contributed. Otherwise, they had to be fought. Tribute would have been the punishment for not believing the truth, and killing for not accepting the punishment. Muslims usually say that tribute was for the Islamic army which protected the non-Islamic members of the community. The verse gives its own reasons.

The command to fight the people of the Book abrogated an earlier command which allowed pardon and forgiveness (2:109). The abrogated verse came when the Muslims were dejected after the battle of Uhud. The abrogating verse came when they were strong to go on the warpath again.

Imam Malek saw that tribute can be taken from those who associate partners with God. As-Shafi'i said that such should be killed.[2] As-Shafi'i's opinion agrees with the verses under study. All men are not born Muslims. It is not practical that they will adopt Islam. The implication of this doctrine is that God gives life to the people of the Book, so that Muslims can take it away. Some say that the people of the Book should be fought; others say that they should be tolerated. There is much confusion in the minds of Muslims about such matters, because they have not accepted what the *Qur'an* says clearly. Muhammad married Mariam, the Coptic girl, and chose Safiyyah the Jewess as soon as he laid his eyes on her. She was married. Her husband was killed when Muhammad defeated the Jews of Khaybar. If Muslims may marry the people of the Book, should they regard them as their enemies?

"There is no compulsion in religion" (2:256). Several interpretations of the verse exist. They have to do either with the Arab children who were attached to Jewish mothers before Islam and who accompanied them when they were expelled from Arabia, or with the case of a Muslim who complained to Muhammad that his sons adopted Christianity. Others said that the verse was abrogated: "O Prophet, struggle with the unbelievers and hypocrites and be harsh with them: their refuge is Jehannam [hell], an evil destination" (9:73). Others said that the people of the Book should not be compelled to submit to Islam as long as they paid tribute. A fifth explanation says that those who believe by the sword should not be said to have been compelled. This referred to the aged people of the Book who were taken in the spoils of war.

Such confusion of interpretation is typical regarding verses which seem to give freedom to people of a different religious conviction. The verses are quoted when the tolerance of Islam is proclaimed. The verses that command fighting are ignored. A typical example is found in as-Sayyed Sabeq's *Exposition of the Sunnah*.[3] He confirms the tolerance of Islam and shies away from mentioning any verse which deals with fighting. Confusion is unacceptable when the verses are not ambiguous. "Do not dispute with the people of the Book but with that which is better, except those who do wrong" (29:46). Muhammad frequently called the Jews and Christians to listen to reason (3:63-83; 4:47; 5:68). A genuine conviction of the truth of Islam was to be the means of conversion, not coercion. Yet when the Jews and Christians refused to accept Islam, they were fought.

"Surely, they who have believed and those who have become Jews and Christians and those of the people of the Book who turned to Islam, whoso believes in God and the Last Day, and works righteousness, their wage awaits them with their Lord, and no fear shall be upon them, neither shall they sorrow" (2:62; 5:69). This means that Jews and Christians who remain in their faith, are safe with God. They should not be fought.

A CONTRADICTION?

Very few Muslims know what to believe regarding men and women of other faiths. The *Qur'an* calls the people of the Book worthy in one verse, and calls for war against them in another. It calls for a reasonable approach, then says fight them until they pay tribute. Many writers on the subject and most other people are muddled as to the true interpretation. Many hold a militant view out of ignorance. They are slaves to a false notion, that by killing men and women they serve God.

The voice of reason is found in the non-aggression verse of 2:190. It takes precedence over every other verse because the *Qur'an* associates non-aggression with the character of God. Nothing can make it redundant. It is the only verse which links such matters to God's attributes. Other verses add that God is knowing and wise, but do not say "Do this because God's character demands it." If a Muslim must fight, he must not be an aggressor. Aggression should start with the other party. Fighting means physical fighting. The Muslim has no right to fight those who verbally disagree with Islam, or whose ideas differ from what the *Qur'an* teaches.

BELIEVERS WHO RELENT

"O Believers, whosoever of you turns from his religion, God will assuredly bring a people he loves and who love him, humble towards the believers and strong towards the unbelievers; men who struggle in the path of God: (5:54).

The verse was said of Abu Bakr, according to ar-Razi and other commentators. It uses future terms when it says "will." The measure of faith of the Arabian tribes was seen by their defection after the death of Muhammad. The reason for their defection was that they were coerced into their faith in the first place. They saw their chance to rebel when Muhammad died. Abu Bakr turned them back by the sword. He promised to slay the men, take the women and children captive, and spoil their goods. The Arabs were needed to fight the battles of Islam. It was a political necessity. Have you a right to apply the verse to individuals who turn back from Islam? Cannot Islam cope with apostasy, except by the penalty of death? Surely Muslims have belittled their faith by their attitude to those among them who obey their conscience and turn back. They fear that men will leave Islam in droves if given the liberty to do so. The verse makes a prediction. It lays down no principle.

"Whoever of you turns back from his religion, then he shall die an unbeliever; those are they whose works shall go for nothing in this world and the hereafter; they are the inmates of the fire, therein shall they abide forever" (2:217).

Have you noticed that the *Qur'an* never lays down a rule that they who turn from Islam should be killed? The rule was invented by men. All the *Qur'an* says is that they will die unbelieving, and God will punish them in this world and the next. He will confound their works. They shall not prosper, and at the end will enter the fire. The same is said in 47:25 of those who turned back from fighting. Their enticement was from Satan. They shall suffer the same fate (v.34).

THE CHRISTIAN ATTITUDE

The *Gospel* does not command the sentence of death upon those who disavow Christ. Where love reigns, there can be no vengeance. "And if any man obey not our word by this epistle, note that man and have no company with him, that he may be ashamed. Yet count him not as an enemy, but admonish him as a brother" (2Thes.3:14,15). Even a heretic was not to be harmed: "A man that is an heretic, after the first and second admonition reject; knowing that he that is such is perverted and sins, being condemned of himself" (Tit.3:10,11). A faith should be able to stand without destroying its opponents when it is based upon sound doctrine. Jesus said: "Love your enemies" (Mt.5:44).

When Christ sent his disciples to preach the gospel, he said: "And whosoever shall not receive you, nor hear your word, when you depart out of that house or city, shake off the dust of your feet. Truly I say to you, it shall be more tolerable for the land of Sodom and Gomorrah in the day of judgment that for that city" (Mt.10:14,15; Mk.6:11; Lk.9:5; 10:11). The punishment for not receiving Christ would thus be exacted on the judgment day. When Paul and Barnabas were rejected by the Jews in the Greek cities, "they shook the dust of their feet against them." (Acts 13:51). The significance of such an act meant that those who rejected Christ brought their desolation upon themselves. This is a statement of Christian tolerance. Do not condemn Christ for what men have done. Those who abused others in his name are his enemies. He will reject them on the judgment day and will refuse to know them.

SUMMARY

Liberty of the conscience is God's gift to men. No man has been given the rule over another's mind. There is a liberty which is not known in Islam due to misinterpretation of the *Qur'an*. The basic principle of behaviour towards unbelievers and men of other religions is the principle of non-aggression (2:190). Muslims are confused about this issue and agitate for the use of force. They have not grasped the clear principle. God is the judge of all men. He will reward each according to his faith or lack of it on the judgment day. The *Qur'an* never calls for the persecution of those who turn from Islam. Who gave you the right to execute the judgment of God? The militancy toward such betrays a fear that many will depart from the faith if given the liberty of exercising their free will. It shows a lack of confidence of Muslims in their own doctrines. When men are not allowed to think or speak according to their own conscience, then bondage, will spread throughout society. The nation becomes chained by tradition and its sons are not free.

References

1. Al-Bukhari, vol.6 pp.78,79.
2. Al-Qurtubi's commentary on the *Qur'an*.
3. As-Sayyed Sabeq, Fiqh us-Sunnah, (Dar ul-Kitab el-'Arabi, Beirut, 1985). vol.2, pp.604,605.

Chapter Fifteen
Principles of Human Behaviour

A few subjects where the Qur'anic and Biblical viewpoints differ, will be discussed.

WINE DRINKING

The argument against wine drinking is simple. Trouble and distress arise in society as a result of drink, therefore drinking should be prohibited. Most problems arise out of the drinking of strong alcoholic drinks, which should be banned.

The *Qur'an* permitted drinking at first and said that wine has uses for men, but its sin is greater than its usefulness (2:219). The next word forbade praying when drunk (4:43) and, finally, wine was forbidden altogether as of the works of the devil (5:90). The usefulness of wine is a stated fact. Many Christians are abolitionists and view wine with the same fear as does the *Qur'an*. The book of Proverbs says: "Wine is a mocker, strong drink is raging: and whosoever is deceived thereby is not wise." (Pr.20:1). "Look not upon the wine when it is red. . . It bites like a serpent and strikes like an adder. Your eyes shall behold strange women, and your heart shall utter perverse things" (Pr.23:31-35). "It is not for kings to drink wine; neither for princes strong drink lest they drink and forget the law and pervert the judgment of any of the afflicted" (Pr.31:4,5). The case against wine is strong.

Jesus drank and was labelled as a wine drinker by his enemies

(Mt.11:19; Lk.7:34). He turned water into wine at a marriage feast (Jn.2:1-11). He instituted the service of remembrance of his death by bread and wine: the wine to represent his blood shed for many (Mt.26:26-29; Mk.14:23; Lk.22:20).

Galatians 5:19-21 lists the sins of the flesh, of which are "envyings, murders, drunkenness, revellings and such like: of which I tell you, as I have told you in time past, that they that do such things shall not inherit the kingdom of God." Drunkenness is placed with murder and other vile crimes. The important principle is that while drunkenness is a sin, wine drinking is not. Excess is a sin, but not moderation. The opposite of gluttony is not the abolition of eating, nor does sexual immorality mean the abolition of the sexual act. Why then is the opposite of excessive drinking abolition?

NOTHING IS WRONG OF ITSELF

Every lawful deed, if carried to excess, becomes a sin. Prayer is not sinful, but if you neglect your duty when praying, you sin by your praying. Alms-giving is not sinful, but if your family goes hungry, you sin by your giving. Killing is not wrong of itself, as demonstrated by judicial killing, but murder is a sin. To defend your country when it is invaded is not wrong, while aggressive warfare is wrong. When legitimate things are used improperly, sin is committed. Drunkenness falls into this category. Notice that the *Qur'an* said that wine has uses. This means that it is not wrong of itself. The *Qur'an* did not lay down a punishment for drunkards. Umar ibn el-Khattab used to beat them with stripes.[1] Wine is forbidden in the garden to those who drink it on earth.[2]

THE CHRISTIAN ATTITUDE

Drunkards shall not inherit the kingdom of God. A Christian is forbidden to keep company with a drunkard who professes faith (1Cor.5:11). The tribe of Ephraim was threatened by God for its pride and drunkenness (Is.28:1-4). "Be not drunk with wine wherein is excess, but be filled with the Spirit" (Eph.5:18). This follows the principle: "You have been called to liberty, only use not liberty for an occasion to the flesh" (Gal.5:13). The Christian view is logical in that it recognizes moderation to be the opposite of excess.

Paul laid down another principle, namely the subjugation of the Christian to Christ. "All things are lawful for me, but I will not be brought under the power of any" (1Cor.6:12). He gave the spiritual reason behind the statement in verse 15: "Do you not know that your bodies are members of the body of Christ?" He used the example of fornication, but the principle applies to the abuse of the body with wine. The ultimate reason is given in verse 20: "For you are bought with a price, therefore glorify God in your body and spirit, which are God's." The Christian is bought with the blood of Christ. He does not belong to himself.

The bishops and deacons of the Church should not be given to wine (1Tim.3:3,8). Excess of wine is listed among the things from which Christians were delivered (1Pet.4:3). Wine gladdens the heart of man, says Psalm 104:15. God gives us all things to enjoy, but "let your moderation be known to all men" (Phil.4:5).

Another reason for not drinking is when it causes a weaker brother in the faith to become a drunkard (Ro.14:20,21). The Christian should deny himself for the sake of his brothers in Christ.

USURY

Usury is lending for a premium. There are two aspects to it: borrowing out of necessity, and borrowing for profit. The *Qur'an* deals with the first aspect only.

BORROWING OUT OF NECESSITY

The verses in the *Qur'an* which forbid usury are mainly 2:275-278; 3:130; 4:161; 30:39. The reason for 2:278 was a personal one. A needy man asked 'Uthman bin 'Affan and al-'Abbas bin abd el-Muttalib to let him have part of their share of dates in order to feed his family. When the time for repayment came, they asked for more than they agreed upon, though interest was included. Other reasons were that the tribes practised usury.[3,4]

Usury in cases of need is exploitation. This is what the *Qur'an* was anxious to eradicate. Muslims applied the principle erroneously to economic policies with consequent stale economies.

Usury is forbidden in the *Bible*, when it takes advantage of the needy. "If you lend money to any of my people that is poor, you shall not be to him as a usurer, neither shall you lay upon him usury. If you at all take your neighbour's raiment to pledge, you shall deliver it to him by the time the sun goes down: for that is his covering only it is his raiment for his skin: wherein shall he sleep? And it shall come to pass when he cries to me, that I will hear, for I am gracious" (Ex.22:25-27). It is clear that a man must not increase his fellow's burden. God will take the side of the oppressed.

Lev.25:35-37 says the same thing, but adds: "If your brother be waxen poor and fallen in decay with you, then you shall relieve him: though he be a stranger, or a sojourner: that he may live with you." The point is not only that usury is forbidden, but also that help must be given to the needy. Nehemiah made the usurers restore the lands they have taken (Neh.5:11). Psalm 15:5 blesses the man who does not put his money to usury.

BORROWING FOR PROFIT

Deut.23:19,20 forbid usury among one's people, but permits it with strangers. The verse implies that there is no hardship. Deut.23 deals with borrowing for convenience. Jesus told a parable of a man who gave his servants money to trade on his behalf before he went on a far journey. He found on his return that two had doubled his money, but the third buried it and returned it as it was. His master said: "You should have therefore put my money to the exchangers [bank, in Luke], and then at my coming, I should have received mine with usury" (Mt.25:14-30 Lk.19:12-27). The parable is about faithfulness in the use of the gifts which God has given us.

Usury is mentioned because it is a proper way of using money where there is no hardship. A man who will borrow from you in order to expand his business will use your money and perhaps lose it. You could be using it in your business. It is right to take a premium to safeguard your possession. The borrower will not be too rash in wasting it, if he knows that he has to return it with interest. The banks buy money for less than they sell it or exchange it, on the same principle. They lend it for more than they borrow it. They are not philanthropic societies, but businesses with overheads and employees. The trouble with society is that people buy what they cannot afford, and borrow for the purpose. It is an abuse of the principle of borrowing. An exception may be made for the purchase of a house, since a man may never be able to save enough to keep up with rising house prices.

KILLING

The heinousness of murder is not only that irreparable injury is done to the victim and his family, but that it is a great insult to God.

The *Qur'an* forbids murder. Murder disrupts the unity of mankind. "Whoso slays a soul, not to retaliate for a soul slain nor for corruption done in the land, shall be as if he had slain mankind altogether" (5:32). Judicial killing is permitted for murder and for corruption in the land. "And slay not the soul God has forbidden, except by right" (17:33).

The *Bible* regards murder as a crime against God. This should be sufficient reason not to commit the act. "Whoso sheds man's blood, by man shall his blood be shed, for in the image of God made he man" (Gen.9:6). Killing defaces the image of God which is found in man. Death was even required of animals if they caused bloodshed: "And surely your blood of your lives will I require; at the hand of every beast will I require it, at the hand of every man, at the hand of every man's brother will I require the blood of man" (Gen.9:5). The punishment of death for murder was pronounced.

THE SANCTITY OF LIFE

When God forbids murder, he also means the preservation of life. Man was created with features that resembled his maker. He was equipped for the office of a Khalifah. God said, "let us make man in our image, after our likeness" (Gen.1:26). He was God's masterpiece. This emphasized the wickedness of murder. Adam's sin was enormous in that it introduced into the earth the seeds of the destruction of God's image.

The story of Cain and Abel stresses the importance which God gave to the sanctity of life. The *Qur'an* mentions the murder, and concludes from it the unity of the race (5:27-31); it advises mutilation for fighting against God and his messenger (5:33). The *Bible* takes a different angle altogether. It stresses the sanctity of life (Gen.4:3-15).

When Adam sinned the ground was cursed for his sake (Gen.3:13-16). In Cain's case, he was cursed from the ground: "Your brother's blood cries unto me from the ground, and now you are cursed from the ground which has opened its mouth to receive your brother's blood from your hand. When you till the ground, it shall not henceforth yield to you her strength; a fugitive and a vagabond you shall be in the earth. And Cain said unto the Lord, my punishment is greater than I can bear, behold, you have driven me out this day from the face of the earth and from your face shall I be hid and I shall be a fugitive and a vagabond in the earth; and it shall come to pass that every one that finds me shall kill me. And the Lord said unto him: therefore whosoever slays Cain shall vengeance be taken on him sevenfold. And the Lord set a mark upon Cain, lest any finding him should kill him" (Gen.4:10-16).

You may be surprised that God did not kill Cain but preserved his life. He was showing that even the murder's life is sacred, and not to be regarded as an object of bloodshed and destruction. His case safeguards against anyone thinking that life was cheap and expendable. Cain was the first murderer on earth. There was no precedent. God wanted to impress upon men the evil of murder. Cain was an example to all. They were to see him, a cursed man, and know the wickedness of his crime. When God threatened to kill anyone who killed Cain, it would be because the killer would repeat the crime. This was to show the new race that even the murder of a murderer is not excused. Thus was the sanctity of life emphasized.

The evil of abortion has exceeded all bounds. It is associated with moral declension. There is no greater degradation to which a nation can reach than to kill its unborn children.

MARRIAGE AND DIVORCE

Certain laws were laid down in history; others on the day of creation. The latter are called Creation Ordinances. Marriage falls into this category.

"And we said, O Adam dwell with your wife in the garden" (2:35; 7:19). "O People, fear God who created you from one being, and created from it its spouse" (4:1). Adam was provided with one wife. This was a creation ordinance, and lays down the rule for successive behaviour. It is the pattern of God's order in his creation. The *Qur'an* breaks this rule and allows a multiplicity of wives, concurrently. "If you fear that you will not act justly towards the orphans, marry such women as seem good to you, two, three, four; but if you fear that you will not be equitable, then only one, or what your right hands own" (4:3). Although some argue that one wife is meant because men will not be equitable (4:129), four wives are permitted in the verses. The privilege is denied to women, who effectively remain inferior to men. Marriage is for love and contentment (30:21). The woman is not a chattel, but "they are garments to you, and you are garments to them" (2:187). Consultation between the two should be even regarding weaning (2:233). A dispute between the husband and wife should be settled, even through their families (4:35,128). The wife should not be hated. A wife has a share of her husband's inheritance (4:12).

POLYGAMY

One pair was sufficient to populate the earth. If God intended polygamy, he would have created four wives for Adam. Those who argue for polygamy are deluded into thinking that a man's sexual urge is greater than a woman's. Men are not satisfied with even four, and still seek their pleasure elsewhere. Women are forbidden to do the same. Adultery will be charged against them. It is said that women outnumber men, especially in times of war. Social conditions therefore govern the principles of marriage. How can contentment, love and mercy (30:21) be found in polygamy? Muslim women are indoctrinated to accept their lot. But they fear their fate. If polygamy is right for one party, it is right for the other. There is no spiritual, biological or moral reason why this should not be the case. If a man is not an adulterer when he marries more than one woman, then neither is a woman if she were to marry more than one man.

Marriage is a union between two partners in a most intimate sense. The fruit of the union is seen in the production of offspring. If a man has children of two wives, then a strange situation occurs in the home. The children are related through the father, but the children of one wife are biological strangers to the other wife. The unity of the marriage is broken.

If marriage is for the performance of the sexual act and the production of offspring only, then there is no difference between the state of man and that of a dog or any other animal. When God brought to Adam his wife, he said, "This is now bone of my bones and flesh of my flesh: she shall be called Woman, because she was taken out of Man. Therefore shall a man leave his father and his mother and shall cleave unto his wife: and they shall be one flesh" (Gen.2:23,24). A man or a woman is not complete, in a sense, without the other. A union exists between them in marriage, which is broken with the entry of a third party in the field. A man cannot be united to two women at the same time, otherwise they are united through him to each other. "For the woman who has one husband is bound by the law to her husband as long as he lives: but if the husband be dead, she is loosed from the law of her husband" (Ro.7:2). The law is not the law of Moses, but the law of the creation ordinance.

The union in marriage is a pattern of the unity of God. Man represents God in his own family, as the provider, keeper and protector. Polygamy is like associating partners with God. Man is fragmented if he is shared. Marriage is also a pattern of the unity of God with his people. God speaks of Jerusalem and says: "Now when I passed by you, and looked upon you, behold your time was the time of love; and I spread my skirt over you and covered your nakedness: yes, I took an oath, and entered into a covenant with you, says the Lord, and you became mine" (Ezek.16:6-8). Jerusalem committed a crime in worshiping other gods. He said, you are "as a wife that commits adultery, who takes strangers instead of her husband" (v.32). But God, the faithful husband returns to her after her punishment, and says: "I will remember my covenant with you in the days of your youth" (v.60). The same is said of the Church. It is the bride of Christ (Rev.21:2). This is why a man must love his wife as

"Christ also loved the church and gave himself for it" (Eph.5:23). Marriage is the pattern of the spiritual union between God and his people. Polygamy is akin to idolatry. "Your Maker is your husband, the Lord of hosts is his name, and your redeemer" (Is.54:5).

Polygamy was practised in ancient times, even by the prominent men of the *Old Testament*. But this was a departure from the pattern which God laid down on the day of creation.

DIVORCE

Divorce breaks the unity found in marriage between a man and a woman, as does adultery. According to the *Qur'an* a woman who is divorced may not be remarried to her husband before she marries another man and is divorced of him (2:230). This is in contrast to divorce under the law of Moses, which said that the woman may not be married again to her husband (Deut.24:1-4). People were not to enter in and out of marriage at their whim. Divorce was permitted because of the hardness of the heart of people, "but in the beginning it was not so," said Jesus (Mt.19:3-12). It was a way by which God controlled the evil which the children of Israel were intent on doing. Divorce is not permitted to the true Christian, apart from the cause of adultery. It was regarded by Jesus as an occasion for adultery. A man who divorces, apart from the reason of adultery, commits adultery with his new wife, and she with him. Divorce may be permitted in the nation for the prevention of greater evil in society.

True believing Muslims, like Christians, should be able to keep the law of God which he initiated at the beginning. The Muslim woman has another disadvantage. She not only fears polygamy, but she fears divorce. This is why Muslim women hoard gold and jewellery, because these may not be taken from them in case of divorce (2:229).

References

1. Malek bin Anis, Kitab ul-muwatta' (Dar ul-Afaq ul-Jaddedat, Beirut, 1983), p.730
2. Ibid; p.732.
3. Al-Wahidi, Asbab nuzool el-Qur'an, p.87
4. As-Suyuti in Makhloof's version of the Qur'an, p.69.

Chapter Sixteen

The Final State of Man

THE RESURRECTION OF THE BODY

Both the *Qur'an* and the *Bible* teach the resurrection of the body for judgment. The soul of man leaves his body after death, and is reunited with it on the resurrection day. The resurrection is not an ingathering of spirits. "Does not man reckon that we shall not gather his bones? Yea, we are able to shape his fingers" (75:3,4). The skin is roasted, because it will cover the suffering body (4:56). A short treatise on the subject of bodily resurrection is provided by 1 Corinthians, Chapter 15. Paul reprimands those who do not believe it.

The resurrection is an act of God. Christ linked it with his return to earth as the judge of all men (Jn.5:27; Mt.24). It will be decisive and final, and is called the hour (22:7; 7:187; 79:42-46; Mt.24:36). God will be the resurrector, and Jesus and the Spirit (2Cor.1:9; Jn.5:28,29; Ro.8:11), that is the triune God. Christ will be the judge of all men (Jn.5:22; 2Tim.4:1; Ro.2:16; Acts 17:31) "because he is the Son of man" (Jn.5:27). No one can say that God did not understand the difficulties of men and their nature and weaknesses, for Christ is man as well God. History revolves around him. When no man could open the book of history, in John's vision, it was the "Lamb as it had been slain" that "took the book out of the right hand of him that sat upon the throne" (Rev.5:1-7). History unfolded with the breaking of the seals of the book.

THE JUDGMENT

Men do not receive what they deserve in this life. This calls for judgment in the other world. Men treasure up their works for the "day of wrath and the revelation of the righteous judgment of God, who will give to every man according to his deeds" (Ro.2:5,6). "Do those who commit evil deeds think that we shall make them as those who believe and do righteous deeds, equal their living and their dying?" (45:21). "Whoever has done righteousness, it is for the benefit of his soul, and whoever has done evil, it is against it" (45:15). "Whoever has done an atom's weight of good will see it, and whoever has done an atom's weight of evil, shall see it" (99:6-8). God writes in a book all the deeds of men (6:59). Not one mustard seed worth of good is lost (21:47). Men will either enter the garden or heaven, or go to hell.

Anyone who reads the *Qur'an* will realize the certainty of the matter and its decisiveness, until one takes note of surah 7:44-50. A great shadow is cast upon the certainty of the final outcome for all men. According to Muslims, believers can go to the fire if they commit the big sins, such as murder and adultery. After a period of suffering, they will enter the garden. Likewise, if the people of the fire show faith as small as a mustard seed, and say there is no God but God, they will be brought out. If men adopted Islam when their life was threatened on earth, would they not all desire to be delivered from the fire of hell after they have tasted it? They will surely know by then that there is only one God. The idea resembles that of Purgatory in Roman Catholicism.

Verses 7:44-50 tell us of the ramparts between the garden and hell. Men will be placed there, according to most interpreters, when their scales of good and evil balance exactly. They will greet the people of the garden, desiring to enter. Their eyes turn toward those in the fire, and will enter the garden after they see the justice of God. There are four implications of this doctrine.

First, judgment is not decisive. God cannot determine on earth the fate of some. A chance is given them after death.

Second, the fate of some will be determined by a confession of faith. Deeds on earth do not determine the destiny of some.

Third, the state of the soul is not taken into account. Does not God know whether the soul is inclined toward him or not?

Fourth, sin cannot go unpunished. Even the faithful taste the fire. If they deserved it, should they not remain in it? Do the faithful enter the garden with a sinful nature that has been temporarily burnt?

The main criticism of such a state of indecision is that it fails to realize that man is a part of his own sin. He does not stand neutral, while his outstretched hands receive either gold or dust. A man is either a sinner or not. He is not divided into compartments. God is not divided in his purpose either. The uncertainty is reflected in the lives of Muslims who cannot be certain of the garden. It is indeed a sin to be sure of one's eternal destiny, excepting death when fighting on God's side. The *Bible* shuns uncertainty. The Christian knows assuredly that he will be with Christ in heaven.

The idea of eternal damnation is too terrible to contemplate. Some people have preferred an idea of annihilation, but it is not up to them to decide what God will do. Man's spirit does not perish. Its death is eternal, unimaginable misery in a state of banishment from God in a place called hell.

THE ETERNAL DESTINY OF MAN

There are two opposite ultimates: the garden and the fire, or heaven and hell. There is nothing in between. The men of the ramparts of surah 7 appear to be temporary dwellers of that place. The garden is often in the plural in the *Qur'an*.

THE GARDEN

The garden is a place of sensual and physical pleasures similar to those on earth, but heightened and at times exceeded. It is a garden without God, and where there is bloodshed albeit of animal life.

The garden is man-centred. Its dwellers eat and drink and indulge in sex to their hearts' content. "They have a garden beneath which the rivers flow; whensoever they are provided with the provision of fruit they shall say, that is what we were provided with before, and they shall be given a certain semblance and there shall be for them spouses purified; therein they shall dwell forever" (2:25). "They recline upon couches" (36:56) and will drink "a cup from a spring," "not intoxicating, and with wide-eyed maidens restraining their glances as if they were hidden eggs" (37:43-49). They shall have small children, "youths, their own," and women specially created for the men. They shall eat fruit and meat and the flesh of birds (52:17,23; 56:20,21). They shall have wives in tents (55:72). The women shall be made virgins (56:36). Rivers of wine and honey shall be for the sustenance of all (47:15). They shall wear silk, and youths shall go about them, and shall drink of silver vessels (18:31; 55:54; 76:11-21). The garden is more favourable to men than women. Men can have many wives, including the specially created maidens. The women are not spoken of as possessing several husbands or having men specially created for them. The Muslim woman suffers a third disadvantage. She can be one of four in marriage, she can be divorced, and her lot in the garden is not as good as man's.

The pleasures of the garden are, in part, the result of bloodshed. For the flesh of birds to be eaten, there must be slaughter. Fish will also be eaten according to the *Hadith*.[2] The eating of meat on earth was allowed as a result of Adam's sin. It was not so at the creation, when God provided plants to be the food of all creatures, including man (Gen.1:29,30). Adam was placed in a garden of fruit. If there is bloodshed in the garden, then life is mixed with death and the stench of blood. It also indicates that the effects of sin remain in believers. They enter the garden with a nature that has not been purified from corruption.

A place of sensual pleasure is unlikely to be a place where God dwells. His presence in the garden is not mentioned in the *Qur'an*. The angels enter from open gates (13:23; 38:50). God looks on from afar and occasionally says, "Peace" (36:58).

The idea of the garden in the *Qur'an* detracts from the purpose of God in the creation of man. Did God enliven him by his Spirit, and give him attributes similar to his, for nothing? Was not man a friend of God, better than the angels at his creation? The idea that he created man for man's own sake cannot be true. It would have been better for him not to create, since more men will be in the fire than in the garden. Should not man's function to worship God (51:56) be closer in eternity than on earth?

HEAVEN AND HELL

Very little is told us about heaven, because its bliss and joys are more than can be described or appreciated by man in sin. This creation was polluted by sin and will be destroyed. The redeemed will live with God. John saw in his vision "a new heaven and a new earth; for the first heaven and the first earth were gone away; and there was no more sea." "The tabernacle of God shall be with men, and they shall be his people, and God shall wipe away all tears from their eyes, and there shall be no more death, neither sorrow, nor crying, neither shall there be any more pain, for the former things are passed away." (Rev.21:1-4). That God's tabernacle is with men means God will live with men. "And there shall be no more curse, but the throne of God and of the Lamb shall be in it; and his servants shall serve him. And they shall see his face; and his name shall be in their foreheads. And there shall be no night there; and they need no candle; neither light of the sun; for the Lord God gives them light, and they reign forever and ever (Rev.22:3-5). The picture is that of a life with God of incalculable bliss, spoken largely in negative terms because there are no positive words to describe it. It is sufficient that they will be with God and will see his face and enjoy his presence forever, and reign with him as kings.

Paul spoke of an experience where one was caught up into paradise and heard unspeakable words, "which is not lawful for man to utter" (2Cor.12:4). Such is the glory of heaven. It is a place of rest (Heb.4:9), worship (Rev.19:1) and eternal life (Mt.25:46). For this reason, those who will enter heaven will be raised with pure, incorruptible and spiritual bodies, with no taint of sin (1Cor.15).

Hell is a place of "everlasting fire prepared for the devil and his angels" and ungodly accursed men (Mt.25:41). It is a place of "wailing and gnashing of teeth" (Mt.13:42), "where their worm dies not and the fire is not quenched" (Mk.9:44,46); a place of "outer darkness" (Mt.8:12; 22:13; 25:30), far from the presence of the Lord.

There is no bloodshed in heaven. The idea of bloodshed is hideous. There is no marriage (Mt.22:30; Mk.12:25; Lk.20:35). This is logical, since God instituted marriage for the completion of the human race. No one will be born in eternity, nor will there be sexual intercourse for its own sake.

CAN MAN ENTER THE GARDEN OR HEAVEN BY HIS GOOD DEEDS?

When Adam was punished, his repentance did not annul his punishment. How can you think that a good deed can erase an evil deed? How can deeds erase the need for punishment? They have no function whatsoever in this domain.

God is known as "severe in punishment" or "terrible in retribution" (40:22; 7:167) and "of painful retribution" (41:43). The Shari'ah can be said to be the sum total of religion, including the doctrines of faith (42:13,21; 5:48). Its legal aspect is based upon external matters. It cannot therefore judge what is in the heart. It demands a penalty when an evil is done, but leaves the sins of the heart—such as envy, hatred and lust—untouched. Mercy is not the function of any law. Mercy comes from God outside the law. The law condemns, and by definition cannot justify. God showed mercy to Adam, but not to the devil. God's law or the Shari'ah judges that the heart is guilty, but has no provision for its physical punishment. The soul must be taken into account on the day of judgment. It is the source of man's actions that come to fruition. Judgment according to deeds involves the reason behind the deeds. If you give alms to be well thought of, or to buy favour with God, or to salve your conscience, or to feel good, your deed is not accepted. Man is a unit, and not only a body to be punished for its deeds. The terror of hell is not only physical, but spiritual misery of untold measure. "Fear God: God surely knows what is in the breasts" (5:7). "He knows the treachery of your eyes, and what the breasts conceal" (40:19; 11:5; 64:4). How can the law punish what is concealed? How can a man be justified by his deeds when his soul cries out against him?

God also judges man according to his nature, for his deeds arise from it. A man's nature is an essential part of his being. It is in a state of sin. You may object that you cannot help your nature. Have you been forced to do the wrong that you have done? The least sin defiles you. A small blot of ink on the breast of your white shirt spoils the shirt. How much more if the shirt is filthy by its very nature?

If God is One, then his law is one. To fall short of the least of his commands is to disobey his law. There are no gradations in disobedience. This point is not appreciated by Muslim theologians. When God's Oneness is affirmed and his law is divided, the implication is that God is divided. If the law of God is the means of entering the garden, then all men must go to hell. The *Bible* speaks of two books that will be opened on the judgment day: The Book of Works and The Book of Life. The Book of Works shall see that all men are condemned to hell, for all have sinned against God. But, "whosoever was not found written in the Book of Life was cast into the lake of fire" (Rev.20:12,15). Those whose names are in the Book of Life are those who have been redeemed by the death and resurrection of Christ.

What, then, is the function of the law? The law defines sin. Had God not forbidden Adam the tree, he could have eaten from it. The commandment defined the transgression: Sin is the transgression of the law" (1Jn.3:4). "By the law is the knowledge of sin. Where there is no law, there is no sin" (Ro.3:20; 4:15). The law defines what is wrong, and sin is disobedience of the law.

The law also aggravates sin. Our nature makes us do what is forbidden. This did not apply to Adam, who was holy at the start. Adam's temptation came from without, through the devil. Ours comes from within and without. Since the law's demands must be fulfilled, it also engenders fear and bondage. A man who cannot do what the law forbids is in bondage to the law. He is free if he desires from his heart to do what the law commands and to shun disobedience. The problem is not with the law, but with our sinful nature. It is like good seed sown in foul ground. Being an expression of God's character, the law is good. But we play havoc with it.

Since the law defines sin and exposes it and condemns it, it cannot possibly be a means of deliverance. Red paint paints the canvas red. It cannot make it white at the same time. This is why it is wrong to think that if you keep Ramadan or the Haj, all your sins will be forgiven. Each duty answers for itself, and never for another. If it is broken, it stands to condemn the offender. How can it remove an offence already committed, when it demands that itself be fulfilled?

The law magnifies the justice of God by demanding punishment. Mercy is by God's pleasure, but not to destroy the justice demanded by the law. In this respect we see the most basic failure of Islam. When God's mercy overcomes his justice, God is divided against himself. One of his attributes vanquishes another. This can never be if God is to remain God. God can never waive punishment and be true to his nature. Both justice and mercy must be satisfied. This is why we can never enter heaven or the garden on the grounds of his law, because God is bound by his own being to execute judgment and send the sinner to hell. By this we see the most important function of the law. It is to show us our helplessness and condemnation, and point us to Christ. In Christ alone did God satisfy his justice and mercy at the same time. There was no other way.

SUMMARY

The resurrection of the dead in bodily form precedes the judgment day. Men are judged according to their works. This includes the driving motives behind the works, that is the state of the heart and the state of our nature. We stand condemned before God. All of us have broken God's law.

The Qur'anic view of the garden is a place of carnal pleasure, where there is the killing of birds for food, and where God is not present. The Christian concept of heaven is of eternal life of bliss in the presence of God.

The way of access to heaven can never be through the law, that is through good works. God's law is a unit and must be obeyed without one single transgression. If this is not the case, then God is not One because his law is an expression of his character. The law defines sin and exposes it; it therefore cannot remove it. Its demand for punishment cannot be waived, otherwise God is not true to himself. God cannot show us mercy unless the demands of the law are satisfied. If his mercy overcomes his justice, then he is divided against his own nature, and is no longer God. The only way by which God could satisfy his mercy and justice is through Jesus Christ.

References

1. As-Sayyed Sabeq, Al-'aqa-id el-Islamiyyat, p.295.
2. Al-Bukhari, vol.6, p.23.

Chapter Seventeen

The Way Back to God

How can a man gain the favour of God and enter heaven? There are certain obstacles that have to be overcome. Adam was thrown out of the garden for his disobedience. Enmity based in selfishness entered his nature, which became polluted by sin. It is reasonable to say that he had to regain a holy nature, be rid of sin and its influence, and pay the penalty which God demanded. Muslims fail to recognize the vital importance of this issue. They depend upon a confession of faith, and good deeds and ritual. How can such matters deliver them from the harm which sin has produced?

MAN'S HELPLESSNESS

Confession of faith in God or Muhammad is not enough: "The devils also believe and tremble" (Jas.2:19). God is not satisfied with lip service. He who confesses God and Muhammad, believes Muhammad's message. Faith in Christ means faith in his redemptive work.

Religious duties are not enough. Duties performed cannot cover duties lapsed. If you do not steal, it does not cover your sin of lying. Similarly if you pray and give alms and do good deeds, you do not answer for misdeeds done. Otherwise, you may do what you please, and then perform certain religious duties. This makes mockery of religion and of God.

Obedience to God's law does not help. The law is one and demands that it never be broken. The need for forgiveness proves this. Adam ate of a tree and brought misery upon himself and mankind.

What of the polluted nature that must be made holy? Can fasting, pilgrimage or any ritual that you can imagine change it? What of your guilt? Can you stand before God and say, not guilty? If you can, why do you hope that he will show you mercy?

What of the punishment for your guilt? Do you expect God to waive it and break his word that he punishes the guilty? Did he not punish Adam for the seemingly smallest offence possible? Remember that the real punishment is hell.

Who of us can thus stand and say to God, "I deserve heaven, let me in?"

GOD'S DILEMMA

Enmity exists between God and the sinner. Man, by nature, loves sin and hates the things of God. Why is God an enemy of unbelievers? (2:98; 41:19,28). It is because he is the enemy of all men who have not received his favour.

God's dilemma was how to reconcile his love and mercy with his justice. His nature demands the punishment of the offender for all eternity. His compassion makes him desire to save the sinner. How could he save him and condemn him to hell at the same time? Only God could find the answer. As Adam represented his progeny and failed on their behalf, so could another representative bear their punishment, renew their nature, remove their guilt, fulfil the demands of God's law, and effect reconciliation with God by removing the enmity.

THE NEED FOR A MEDIATOR

The idea of a mediator is not foreign to the *Qur'an*. Its emphasis is not reconciliation. The Qur'anic mediatorship or pleading or speaking on behalf of another to God occurs on the judgment day on behalf of the godly (10:3; 40:18, 74:48) and by the permission of God (20:109; 34:23). There is hardly any need for a mediator for the godly. They should have nothing to fear. The true mediator is the one who brings two conflicting parties together. He is not someone who says to God, forget and forgive, or tip the balance in favour of this or that. He must offer to God a sure ground and justification, whereby God may forgive. Job cried: "If I wash myself with snow water and make my hands never so clean, yet you shall plunge me in the ditch, and my own clothes shall abhor me. For he is not a man, as I am, that I should answer him and we should come together in judgment. Neither is there an umpire [arbitrator] between us, that might lay his hand on us both" (Job 9:30-33). He said, "Is there no one to bring us together? Is there no mediator between us?" The only true mediator to satisfy God's demands is Jesus Christ.

THE SECOND ADAM

Paul argues this out in Romans, Chapter 5. He traces the history of mankind in sin, and shows that even before the law of Moses was given, men died. "By one man sin entered into the world, and death by sin; so death passed upon all men, for that all have sinned" (v.12). His argument involved infants, for they also died. The consequences of Adam's sin passed down upon his progeny. His punishment was their punishment. Then comes a second Adam and stands before God as the representative of all whom he would redeem. He has authority with God. He says, "I will represent them. I will deliver all that you require of them. I will save them, and you will let them be free." This man is the mediator between God and men, the man Jesus Christ, the second Adam. Whereas the first Adam failed, the second Adam triumphed. John Henry Newman (1801-1890) said:

> O loving wisdom of our God:
> When all was sin and shame,
> A second Adam to the fight,
> And to the rescue came.

As the sin of Adam was imputed to his seed, so the righteousness of Christ was imputed to those he represented. "For as by one man's disobedience many were made sinners, so by the obedience of one shall many be made righteous;" "that as sin reigned unto death, even so might grace reign through righteousness unto eternal life through Jesus Christ our Lord" (vv.19,21). "There is now therefore no condemnation to them who are in Christ Jesus" (Ro.8:1).

THE QUALITIES NEEDED IN A MEDIATOR

The parties in disagreement are God and man. If God were to be the mediator, it will not be fair to man. If man is to be the one, then he is not independent as far as God is concerned. The mediator must be unbiased. He must be a God-Man.

The mediator must be flawless in his person, not a sinner, or else he would be in the same position as sinful man. He must be able to satisfy God's law by offering total obedience, and by paying the penalty it already demands. He must be able to show the sinner his need of God and to regenerate his nature. He must have authority with God, not to pontificate but to provide the means whereby the demands of God can be met by man. It was God who provided the mediator, Christ Jesus, the second person in the Holy Trinity. If there had been any other way, God would have taken it. The sending of his Son cost him more than we can imagine. The price of redemption was high.

This was the necessity of the incarnation: the Word of God personified as man in the womb of Mary by the Spirit of God without the agency of a man. Jesus entered the synagogue and was given the book of the prophet Isaiah to read. He opened it to the verse that said: "The Spirit of the Lord is upon me, because he has anointed me to preach the gospel to the poor; he has sent me to heal the brokenhearted, to preach deliverance to the captives, and the recovering of sight to the blind, to set at liberty them that are bruised, to preach the acceptable year of the Lord" (Is.61:1,2). "And he closed the book and gave it to the minister and sat down. And the eyes of all were fastened upon him. And he began to say to them: this day is this scripture fulfilled in your ears" (Lk.4:16-21). The closure of the book was against the custom. Jesus did it to emphasize to them that he was the last word of God to man.

THE MEDIATOR AND THE LAW

"When the fulness of time was come, God sent forth his Son, made of a woman, made under the law, to redeem them that were under the law, that we might receive the adoption of sons" (Gal.4:4,5).

The method of the birth of Jesus ensured that he was without sin. Neither the *Qur'an* nor the *Bible* attribute sin to him. Even the *Hadith* supports this. Adam, Noah, Abraham, and Moses confessed their sins on the day that God was very angry. When it came to Jesus, the *Hadith* says specifically that Jesus mentioned no sin.[1] He challenged his hearers: "Which of you convicts me of sin?" (Jn.8:46). He said of the devil before his crucifixion: "The prince of this world comes and has nothing in me" (Jn.14:30).

Jesus fulfilled the law in its entirety. "Think not that I am come to destroy the law or the prophets: I am not come to destroy, but to fulfil. For truly I say to you, till heaven and earth pass, one jot or one tittle shall in no case pass from the law, till all be fulfilled" (Mt.5:17,18).

Jesus came under the condemnation and curse of the law when he offered himself in the place of sinners.

THE WORK OF THE MEDIATOR IS DECLARED BY HIS NAME

Jesus is called Christ Jesus son of Mary in the *Qur'an*. "Christ" is the Greek equivalent of the Hebrew "Messiah." His name was given him by God through the angel.

AL-MASEEH

This is the Arabic term for Messiah. It is not a family name, like Jones in Jack Jones. It is a title. The *Qur'an* places the article "al" for "the" in this title. It is like saying, the Great, or the Conqueror, or the Terrible, for Alexander, William and Ivan, respectively. It is like calling Muhammad the Messenger of God. We have to turn to the *Old Testament* to learn the significance of the term as applied to Jesus.

The Messiah means "the anointed one." His anointing was not with oil, but with the Holy Spirit who came upon him at his baptism of John (Mt.3:16; Mk.1:10; Lk.3:22; Jn.1:33). The *Qur'an* says that he was supported by the Holy Spirit (2:87,253; 5:110). The anointed ones in the *Old Testament* were the king, the prophet and the priest.

God sent Samuel to anoint Saul king over Israel (1Sam.9:16). David, Solomon and other kings were anointed. "But to the Son he says, your throne, O God, is forever and ever: a sceptre of righteousness is the sceptre of your kingdom. You have loved righteousness and hated iniquity; therefore God, even your God, has anointed you with the oil of gladness above your fellows" (Heb.1:8,9; Ps.45:6,7). The Son is a reference to Jesus, who is also God. The epistle to the Hebrews starts by asserting that Jesus was anointed "heir to all things" (Heb.1:2). He was known as the son of David, who as foretold was to sit on the throne of David in a spiritual sense (Is.9:7; Ps.89:4). The genealogies of Matthew and Luke trace him back to David. The word of the angel to Mary regarding him was that "The Lord God shall give him the throne of his father David: and he shall reign over the house of Jacob for ever: and of his kingdom there shall be no end" (Lk.1:32,33). Jesus said: "All power is given me in heaven and in earth" (Mt.28:18). He is called "the blessed, the only Potentate, the King of kings and the Lord of lords" (1Tim.6:15). His function as a king was for "the bringing of many sons to glory" (Heb.2:8-10), that is, to effect their salvation.

Elisha's anointing as a prophet is the only one mentioned in the *Old Testament*. Jesus was a prophet in that he came to say what the Father sent him to say and do. He called himself a prophet, and was known as such (Lk.13:33; Jn.4:44; Mt.13:57).

The priests were anointed and separated for the service of God. God said to Moses: "You shall anoint Aaron and his sons and consecrate them, that they minister to me in the priest's office" (Ex.28:41; 30:30). One of the most important functions of the priests was the offering of sacrifices to God to atone for the sins of the people. The priesthood was of the tribe of Levi. It pointed to the only true Great High Priest of the tribe of Judah, who was to offer himself as a sacrifice for sinners. There could be none other of the tribe but him. The subject of his atonement will be discussed in detail.

JESUS

This is the common name of Jesus, equivalent to the Hebrew "Yeshua" or Joshua. The angel announced to Mary: "You shall call his name Jesus, for he shall save his people from their sins" (Mt.1:21; Lk.1:31). Joshua saved the children of Israel from their enemies and led them to the promised land.

SON OF MARY

Jesus, of no human father, was "the seed of the woman" who was to bruise the serpent's head (Gen.3:15). This was a reference to him immediately after the fall of Adam and Eve into sin. He was to be the saviour who will crush the devil. He was prophesied of in Is.7:14 as the child of a young maiden, a virgin.

THE ATONEMENT

The atonement is the final common pathway of God's justice, mercy and love. Without it there is no access to God, and no hope of heaven. It is an act whereby a worthy, vicarious sacrifice secures life for men. The penalty is borne by the innocent to rescue the guilty.

The atonement is the centre of gravity of the priestly office of Christ. When God determined, before time began, to rescue fallen man, there was no other way to do it. The atonement was the only way by which his justice is satisfied, and his love and mercy shown.

The necessity of the atonement is not in the nature of God. He was not obliged to save man. He could have let him perish. He provided no redemption for the devils. Redemption is of the free will of God and according to his pleasure.

God's power is not limited. Yet he cannot deny himself and contradict his own nature. This is why there was no other way. Those who have a poor view of sin will not appreciate the necessity of the atonement. Sin is not an imperfection, weakness, or forgetfulness to do one's duty toward God. It is a state of lawlessness answerable to the law. Forgiveness was not built into the law. The law says obey and live, disobey and die. When one thinks about the great price God had to pay, one should be amazed at the dire necessity of the atonement. If there was any other way than the humiliation of Christ, to carry sin and die, God would not have ordained the atonement. It was ordained because God, in his great mercy and love could not save men and women by any other means. Through the atonement, God solved the great dilemma. Some have asked why, if man can forgive, cannot God do the same? The answer lies in the nature of sin and the nature of God. God and sin cannot agree.

Like everything else that God does, it is the triune God who works, because God is triune. The Father sent the Son. The Son offered himself voluntarily to be the sacrifice, and the Holy Spirit raised up Jesus from the dead and applies the benefit of his work to those whom he regenerates: "Elect according to the foreknowledge of God the Father, through sanctification of the Spirit, unto obedience of the sprinkling of the blood of Christ" (1Pet.1:2).

THE CONCEPT OF SACRIFICE

God Accepted Sacrifice

The story of the sons of Adam shows us that God accepted sacrifice. "And recite to them the story of the two sons of Adam truthfully, when they offered a sacrifice and it was accepted of one of them and not accepted of the other" (5:27). The *Qur'an* concludes from this incident that men should not kill one another unjustly. The nature of the sacrifice is not told. The phrase "and was accepted of one of them" means that God accepted sacrifice.

The Biblical story tells how Cain offered of the fruit of the earth, and Abel of the fat firstlings of his flock (Gen.4:3-5). Cain did not give his best, and he offered vegetables. Abel gave of his best and it was a sacrifice of blood. Although the spiritual state of the offerer is important in the story, it is the blood that was the most significant. How did Abel know that this was what God wanted? Adam and Eve were still alive at the time. They must have received a word from God about the matter. Abel obeyed the instructions of God and Cain did not. When the sons of Aaron offered strange incense before the Lord, they were consumed by fire

(Lev.10:1,2). The conclusion is that sacrifice had to be done with a clean heart and it had to be a blood sacrifice.

God Demanded Sacrifice

The story of Abraham and his son tells us that God demanded sacrifice. "He said, my son, I see in my sleep that I slay you; consider what you think. He said, my father, do what you are commanded" (37:102-107). "Do what you are commanded" means that God commanded sacrifice. The incident was a trial of Abraham and his son.

"And when Moses said to his people, God commands you to sacrifice a cow" (2:67-74), they asked him about its features. It was to be "with no blemish." The message of the paragraph is that God can raise the dead. The significance of sacrifice must not be ignored. "God commands you to sacrifice" stresses again that God commanded sacrifice. If God can raise the dead, it might be a greater miracle to raise an old cow than a young cow. The reference must be to what God commanded the children of Israel to do, as detailed in the *Bible*.

A whole sacrificial system was set up, with its priesthood, altar, methods and causes for sacrifice. The separation of Aaron and his son for the priesthood (Ex.40:13-33; Lev.8) involved the placing of the blood of a sacrifice upon them (Lev.8:23). Offerings for moral misdemeanour were sacrifices of blood. The burnt offering had to be "without blemish" (Lev.1:3), as was the peace offering (Lev.3:1), the offering for the sin of ignorance (Lev.4), the trespass offering, and the sin offering (Lev.5-7; 16). Sacrifice was the main feature in the life of the children of Israel, offered on behalf of individuals, congregations, priests and the whole people. Lev.16 describes how two goats were to be brought for a sin offering for the people. One was to be a sacrifice, the other a scapegoat. "Aaron shall lay both his hands upon the head of the live goat and confess over it all the iniquities of the children of Israel and all their transgressions in their sins, putting them upon the head of the goat, and shall send it away by the hand of a fit man into the wilderness; and the goat shall bear upon it their iniquities" (Lev.16:21-22). This represented the carrying away of the sins of the people by a victim, while the other victim was sacrificed for atonement. There were daily sacrifices for the people and life was covered by sacrifice.

Before the children of Israel left Egypt, God said that he would strike the firstborn in the land, but would pass over the houses where the blood of a lamb without blemish was painted on the door posts: "When I see the blood, I will pass over you" (Ex.12:13). Death had already taken place in the households covered with the blood. The Passover was to be observed every year. The other annual feast was the Day of Atonement. All the people gathered before the Lord, and a sacrifice was offered to make atonement for their sins (Lev.23:23-33).

God Provided Sacrifice

When God spared Abraham's son, he did not leave the matter at that. He provided a sacrifice in place of Abraham's son. Abraham's son was spared, but a ram caught in the thicket was sacrificed in his stead, according to Gen.22:13,14. The *Qur'an* says of this: "And we ransomed him with a mighty sacrifice" (37:107). When it says "*we*" it means God, that is God ransomed Abraham's son. The ram died, and the son lived. This is the principle of vicarious sacrifice. Christians do not offer sacrifices. Jews should, but do not. Only Muslims offer sacrifices every year. Most do not know the reason why. The Day of the Sacrifice at the end of the Haj is kept in all Islamic lands as the Feast of the Sacrifice. The sacrifice to feed the poor must be offered with a clean heart: "The flesh of them shall not reach God neither the blood, but godliness from you shall reach him" (22:32-38). There must be a more significant reason for killing thousands of sheep than to feed the poor. Many spend their life savings to go on pilgrimage.

The reason must be related to Abraham's sacrifice of a sheep to redeem his son. Muslims believe that Abraham and Ishmael built the Ka'bah. "And we made a covenant with Abraham and Ishmael to purify my house for those who go about it and those that cleave to it and those who bow and prostrate themselves" (2:125). "Abraham, and Ishmael with him, raised the foundation of the house" (2:127). Muslims refuse to accept the significance of vicarious sacrifice, when the *Qur'an* plainly says "And we ransomed him with a mighty sacrifice." They go out of their way to justify unreasonable and meaningless causes. It is said that sacrifices symbolize the "shedding of the blood of the evil thing by the hand made strong by good, and a sign of the willingness to sacrifice in the presence of the righteous host of the Lord." This is a travesty of the truth. The *Qur'an* never gives such a meaning to sacrifice. The *Hadith* adds that past sins will be forgiven if the Haj is carried out properly. Muslims have no real understanding of the meaning of sacrifice.

THE BLOOD

The *Qur'an* forbids the eating of blood (2:173; 5:3; 16:115). The flesh, heart, intestines, stomach, kidneys, pancreas, liver, and even the brain are eaten, so why not the blood? The answer is that the life is in the blood. God said to Noah: "The flesh with its life, which is its blood, you shall not eat." (Gen.9:4). This was reiterated to the children of Israel: "I will set my face against the soul that eats blood;" "for the life of the flesh is in the blood, and I have given it upon the altar to make atonement for your souls: for it is the blood that makes an atonement for the soul" (Lev.17:10-14; 19:26; Deut.12:23; 1Sam.14:32,33; Acts 15:20,29). Bloodshed is synonymous with killing:

> Mind and soul with evil are filled;
> God's image is with one stroke killed:
> The life is drawn; the blood is spilled.

To drain the blood of a creature is to drain its life. Blood was to be the means of the redemption of mankind.

DID JESUS CHRIST DIE?

"And their saying, we slew the Messiah, Jesus the son of Mary, the messenger of God, yet they did not slay him, neither crucified him, but a likeness of him was shown to them. And those who are at variance concerning him, surely are in doubt regarding him, they have no knowledge of him except to surmise, and they slew him not for a certainty, but God raised him up to him, and God was mighty, wise" (4:157,158).

This is a frank denial of the death of Jesus. The Arabic commentaries show different views as to how his likeness occurred. Some said that it was placed on Judas, or one of the guards. Another story told that Jesus asked his disciples who among them would buy the garden by receiving his likeness. One volunteered and was crucified in his place. This suggests that Jesus was involved in a forgery, and that he was not man enough to accept his destiny. Ar-Razi was right in saying that to liken one man to another "opens the gate for Sophism," that is, to fallacious argument. He says: "If we see Zaid, perhaps it is not Zaid, but his likeness, and then there is no confidence in marriage or divorce." He argued that some may limit this impartation of likeness to the prophets. He was astute in concluding that no prophet could be trusted, if it were so, because he could be not he, but another. But note this: if the likeness of Jesus died, then the *Qur'an* implies the doctrine of substitution.

This is not the last word of the *Qur'an*. "And God said, O Jesus, I am causing you to die and lifting you up to myself, and purifying you from those who do not believe and making your followers above those who did not believe until the Resurrection Day; then to me is your return and I will judge between you in what you were disputing" (3:55). Jesus said: "I was a witness while I was with them, and when you caused me to die, you yourself were a watcher over them" (5:117).

The words "mutawaffeeka" and "tawaffaytani," used for "causing to die," have been said to mean "to complete," or "completed my days on earth." Christ will return, kill the false Christ and then will die according to Muhammad's saying.[3,4]

The idea of death is stated sooner or later in interpretation. The meaning is that God will take the souls to himself, or grasp their spirit. It is the sole meaning in the dictionary of *al-Fairuz Abadi* and the predominant one in *Lisan ul-Arab*. The verb "yatawaffakum," meaning "to cause you to die," refers to more than two people. "He is the one who 'yatawaffakum' in the night" (6:60). "I worship God who will 'yatawaffakum'" (10:104). The word is taken on both occasions to mean "cause you to die." Commentators, such as ar-Razi and al-Qurtubi, mentioned what early Muslims said of the word with reference to Jesus. Ibn Zaid, and al-Hasan, and ibn Jareeh said, the word "mutawaffeeka" means "grasping your spirit," which is the same as "taking you up." The spirit of Jesus was grasped. The idea of death is inevitable. Others said that the death of Christ was meant. Wahab bin Manbah said that Christ died in three hours, then was lifted up. Ibn al-Abbas and Muhammad ibn Ishaq said that Jesus took seven hours to die, then God raised him up and lifted him to himself. Others said that he died at the point of being lifted to heaven. This shows that the idea of the death of Jesus was paramount in the interpretation of the Qur'anic verses.

If Jesus had not died and risen again, there would have been no Christianity. The people who preached the gospel saw him alive, and talked with him and ate with him after he rose from the dead. They saw his empty tomb, the nail marks in his hands, and the spear scar in his side. Why do you think that they could not but turn the world upside down with their message? The *Gospel* is not based on speculation, but on eyewitness accounts of what happened. Can you imagine that God raised the likeness of Jesus to further perpetrate a deception? The accusation reaches the gates of heaven. When the disciples preached the resurrection, men could check for themselves whether the body of Jesus was in the tomb or not.

THE DEATH OF JESUS AS RECORDED

Crucifixion was a slow form of death. Yet Christ died much more quickly than the thieves, though he was not physically weaker than they. When Joseph of Arimathaea begged the body of Jesus from Pilate,

"Pilate marvelled if were dead already" (Mk.15:44). The soldiers came to take the men down to break their legs, before Passover Sabbath day, so that they could die of circulatory collapse. But Jesus was dead already. "But one of the soldiers with a spear pierced his side, and forthwith there came out blood and water. And he that saw it bare record, and his record is true, and he knows what he says is true, that you might believe" (Jn.19:34,35). This was the eyewitness account of John. He recorded the strange event of blood and water because he saw it. A possible explanation is that Jesus' heart ruptured.

When a newly dead body is pierced, blood does not come out with water. If the story was a fabrication, other eyewitnesses would have denied it. There would have been no virtue in telling a lie of an abnormal event. There is a blood test called the Erythrocyte Sedimentation Rate (E.S.R.) which is used to measure the course of inflammatory or rheumatic disease in the body. A small amount of blood is placed in a thin tube and prevented from clotting. The sedimentation rate of the blood cells per hour is noted. The blood separates into a lower cellular layer, and an upper plasma layer. This process does not take place after circulation has ceased. Clotting occurs. But if the blood was already outside the system, it could produce a soft clot with serum above it. Jesus was hanging upright on the cross. If his heart ruptured, it would explain the separation of clot and serum to account for what John saw and could not explain. A healthy heart does not rupture, and its covering pericardial membrane is strong. Jesus suffered torment and agony which no man could imagine. He did not fear death, but feared the separation from his Father, when his holy and sinless body bore the sin of the world, as if he committed all the evil that men had done. Such things could not have happened to his likeness; a likeness would have ended with broken legs. Jesus died at the time of the Passover, for he was the Lamb of God who died for the sins of the world (Jn.1:29). Thomas Kelly (1769-1854) described Christ's agony:

> Tell me, ye who hear Him groaning,
> Was there ever grief like His?
> Friends through fear His cause disowning;
> Foes insulting His distress,
> Many hands were raised to wound Him,
> None would interpose to save;
> But the deepest stroke that pierced Him
> Was the stroke that Justice gave.

The justice was the justice of God upon the mediator who accepted the punishment for the sins of those whom he represented.

THE VOLUNTARY DEATH OF CHRIST

Jesus died voluntarily. A mediator would lose his status if he were an unwilling victim. When his hour approached, Jesus went to Jerusalem, knowing that he would be arrested. His disciples followed fearfully (Mk.10:32-34). When Peter tried to defend him, he would not have it: "Do you think that I cannot now pray to my Father and he shall presently give me more than twelve legions of angels? But how shall the scriptures be fulfilled that thus it must be?" (Mt.26:53,54). This is consistent with what he said before: "I am the good shepherd: the good shepherd gives his life for the sheep. I lay down my life that I might take it again. No man takes it from me, but I lay it down of myself" (Jn.10:12-18). He said that he came "to give his life a ransom for many" (Mt.20:28; Mk.10:45). Even when he prayed in the garden of Gesthemane, "not my will but yours be done" (Mt.26:42), he voluntarily submitted to the Father's will. "Having loved his own who were in the world, he loved them unto the end" (Jn.13:1).

ATONEMENT AND THE COVENANT OF GOD

The covenant of God with men is the basis of his redemption. God placed enmity between the seed of the woman and the devil after our first parents fell (Gen.3:15). He did not destroy the whole of mankind in the flood, for the redeemer had to come from the same seed. He promised Abraham, Isaac and Jacob that in their "seed shall all the nations of the earth be blessed." This seed did not refer to the children of Israel, but to Christ (Gal.3:16). When God made a covenant with the children of Israel, they said, "All that the Lord has said we will do and be obedient." The covenant was ratified with blood and the people were sprinkled with the blood (Ex.24:7,8). God was to be their God. They could not keep his covenant. Revelation progressed through history, until God promised them a new covenant when he would put his law in their hearts and they would know him (Jer.31:31-34). This new covenant was sealed with the blood of Christ. The blood of the old covenant pointed to Christ's own, which was to be shed for his people. Jesus asked his disciples to remember his death: "This cup is the new testament in my blood which is shed for you" (Lk.22:20). The revelation of God is bathed in the blood of sacrifices which pointed to the supreme and true sacrifice of Jesus. The son of the woman, the same Son of God, "was manifested that he might destroy the works of the devil" (1Jn.3:8). Men would no longer be chained by sin under the influence of the evil one.

A covenant of grace was necessary. Men failed to keep the old covenant, which required total obedience to the law of God. Christ came as a representative of his chosen. He undertook to fulfil the contract on their behalf, and pay the penalty demanded for failing to keep the covenant. God was then under obligation to do his part and give them the blessings of the covenant. The "surety" or "mediator" of the covenant, Jesus, has ensured this by his obedience and death (Heb.7:15,22). The legal obligations of the covenant were met. He atoned for sin by his sacrifice, and brought men out of the bondage of the law and its punishment. Whereas the old covenant required sacrifices day after day, the sacrifice of Jesus was once for all time, sufficient for all the demands of God, for ever (Heb.9), confirmed by his resurrection from the dead.

ONE SACRIFICE

The repetition of the sacrifices of the Haj, as was the case with the sacrifices of the Levitical priesthood, proves their insufficiency. One bath or shower does not do for all time. You probably wash your hands several times a day. One wash does not prevent further pollution. Such is the case with sacrifices that have to be offered again and again. Do you think that the blood of a bull, sheep or goat is worthy to cover the soul of man? Is not man of more value than such creatures? The sacrifices could never take away sin. They were signs or pointers to the one true and only real sacrifice of all history. The sacrifice had to be of infinite worth to cover mankind. A perfect man would not do. He had to be a God-Man.

Christ, "after he had offered one sacrifice for sins for ever, sat down on the right hand of God" (Heb.10:4,12). There was no more to be done. As God settled upon the throne after he completed the creation, so did Christ after he completed his work of redemption. The High Priest entered once a year into the holiest part of the tabernacle which represented the presence of God. He had to make an atonement for himself and the people, and dared not enter without blood. But Christ, "by his own blood entered once into the holy place, having obtained eternal redemption for us" (Heb.9:12). The veil which separated the holiest place was torn from the top to the bottom, not by man, but by God, when Jesus died (Mt.27:51; Mk.15:38). This meant that God was pleased with his sacrifice, and that he opened the way for men to come into his presence. Here we see how the mediator effected his mediation: "God was in Christ reconciling the world to himself." "We are reconciled to God by the death of his Son" (2Cor.5:19; Ro.5:10). The enmity between God and man had ended. Man could be the friend of God again. God's Justice and Mercy were satisfied. God remained One, undivided.

Punishment had been meted out and accepted. Mercy could be shown to undeserving sinners. The gates of heaven were open.

THE BENEFITS OF THE ATONEMENT

Man must stand before God and be pronounced "not guilty." It is not enough that he is forgiven. If, according to the Qur'anic concept of balances, man's good deeds weigh fifty-one percent, he enters the garden carrying forty-nine percent of his sins. In other words, man enters the garden in a state of guilt. The only way by which man may become righteous is to be endowed with the righteousness of Christ. As Adam's guilt was imputed to his seed, so the righteousness of Christ is imputed to the redeemed. God sees them robed in righteousness, and has nothing against them.

Human nature was polluted and corrupted by sin. Adam could not be allowed to remain in the garden after he lost his holiness. He would have needed the restoration of his nature. If man enters the garden with his sinful nature, then the garden will be full of enmity, greed, selfishness and all manner of sin. The *Qur'an* hints that the nature of the people of the garden will be renewed: "God will remove rancour from their hearts," that is, envy or secret hatred (7:43; 15:47). You cannot remove envy as you discard or cut out a lump of diseased tissue. It is part of the nature of fallen man.

> The sins which were your drink and bread
> Are part of you: on them you fed.

The nature must, therefore, be renewed. The *Qur'an* provides no basis for or justification of why God should do this. The concept of the second birth is the answer of God to this problem. He renews the nature of the redeemed by giving them new birth by his Spirit. "Except a man be born again, he cannot see the kingdom of God," said Jesus. "That which is born of the flesh is flesh; and that which is born of the Spirit is spirit" (Jn.3:3-7). The renewed man is a child of God by adoption. He is no longer under the wrath of God. He will show the fruit of his new nature. "The fruit of the Spirit is love, joy, peace, longsuffering, gentleness, goodness, faith, meekness, self-control" (Gal.5:22,23). Works acceptable to God follow renewal, never before. The new man will live under the Lordship of Christ in all things. Although the old body will die because of the pollution of sin within it, although its weaknesses will fight against the new nature, it will be redeemed in the end when it is resurrected incorruptible, immortal, and a spiritual body, fashioned like the glorious body of Christ (1Cor.15:44,54; Phil.3:21).

Christ came "to destroy the works of the devil" (1Jn.3:8; Jn. 12:31). The devil no longer has power over believers. "The wages of sin is death; but the free gift of God is eternal life through Jesus Christ our Lord" (Ro.6:23). Death shall be conquered through eternal life (1Cor.15:26,55,56).

THE APPLICATION OF REDEMPTION

What Christ did does not automatically save the whole of mankind. His work has to be applied by the Holy Spirit to men and women. He has to open their dead spiritual eyes so that they can see their position in sin and come to Christ by faith. Faith is the instrument which God uses to apply by his Spirit the work of Christ to them. Faith means complete and total trust in what Christ has done, not in human endeavour, to attain salvation. "The law is not of faith, for the man that does them shall live by them" (Gal.3:12). The law demands obedience, not faith. The kind of faith that is needed is the gift of God (Eph.2:8). A man dead in trespasses and sins (Eph.2:1) must first be given life by the Spirit of God (Jn.6:63; 2Cor.3:6).

As Adam's clay was made alive by the Spirit of God, so the new man is made alive by the same Spirit. Once having been made alive, he cannot but believe, as a positive act on his part, having received the gift of faith. God does not tell us whom he will make alive. He commands us to believe and will judge us if we do not. It is a mystery that God lays the responsibility at our doorstep, yet he holds the key to life and faith.

The plan of salvation was not an afterthought following Adam's sin. The Bible regards Jesus "as the Lamb slain from the foundation of the world" (Rev.13:8). Peter told the people that Christ, who "was delivered by the determinate counsel and foreknowledge of God, you have taken, and by wicked hands crucified and slain." (Acts 2:23). Even Satan was used to enter Judas Iscariot, who betrayed Jesus (Lk.22:3)

> He bled and died with certain knowledge
> That death will flee before his Name;
> Hell and Satan could not envisage
> Their servile action in His aim.

Christ "was truly foreordained before the foundation of the world, but was manifest in these last times" (1Pet.1:20). Men and women were chosen in him "before the foundation of the world" (Eph.1:4). The foreknowledge of God has been discussed already. He is not a crystal-ball-gazer who can read the future. He foreknows because he foreordains, or decides beforehand, according to his sovereign will.

Some may charge God with unfairness. The truth is that no man has a claim on God. We all deserve hell. If God decides to snatch from hell whom he will snatch, it is his will. Has anyone grumbled that God was unfair for deciding to choose people from Adam's progeny, and not to choose the devil and his company? Jesus told a parable of a man who employed labourers to work his field. He agreed with the ones he employed first on a certain wage. He later hired others, and others later still. He paid them the same wage at the end of the day. The first, having worked longer grumbled. The man answered, "Is it not lawful for me to do what I will with my own? Is your heart evil because I am good?" (Mt.20:15). God said: "I will show mercy on whom I will show mercy" (Ex.33:19). Paul uses the verse in Romans 9 and deals with the case of Pharaoh who was shown no mercy. He anticipates the question, "Why does he yet find fault?" Is it Pharaoh's fault for not believing because God showed him no mercy and hardened his heart? He answers, "O Man, who are you to reply against God? Shall the thing formed say to him that formed it, why have you made me thus? Has not the potter power over the clay, of the same lump to make a vessel to honour, and another to dishonour" (vv.19-21). The *Qur'an* teaches the same thing. "He specifies his mercy to whom he wills." "He leads astray whom he wills." "He takes into his mercy whom he wills." "He forgives whom he wills and afflicts whom he wills" (2:105,213,284; 3:72-74,129; 5:18; 14:27 42:8). Many of the verses are not related to man's actions or faith. God's election is free and unconditional. Jesus said, "my sheep hear my voice," and "I give to them eternal life; and they shall never perish, neither shall any man pluck them out of my hand" (Jn.10:27,28). "Nothing can separate those who are in Christ from his love" (Ro.8:37-39). The unbeliever cannot blame God for his unbelief. It is not given to man to pry into the mind of the Almighty. God chooses whom he wills, while man is commanded to believe and is held responsible for his actions.

SUMMARY

No religion or tradition of men has taught the doctrine of vicarious sacrifice for the redemption of sinners by the God who is offended by their sin. Nor has the concept of the Creator dying for his creatures to save them from his own wrath ever been taught, apart from the *Bible*. The gods may die in the winter and rise in the spring. Ashtaroth may weep for her Cadmus, but Cadmus does not die to save men from their sin.

All religions teach that men must do good and shun evil. Human philosophy and common sense teach the same. Religions have failed to appreciate that these means do not achieve forgiveness. They are irrelevant to the vital issue of an offended God whose justice demands satisfaction. The *Bible* is the only book which extols the holiness and justice of God, and shows the incompatibility and heinousness of sin with regard to his nature. It is unique in asserting the true Oneness of God. It does not divide his nature by making one attribute overcome or stifle another. It reveals God's inestimable love, compassion, mercy and justice. By Christ's atonement, his justice and mercy are satisfied, while he remains undivided. His love cannot overcome his holiness, for he is holy love. Atonement by the blood of Jesus was the only way which was open to God to save sinful man. His Oneness prevents him from waiving a punishment deserved. It barred the way to heaven. Atonement satisfies the demands of God's justice. Such is the gravity of sin that it was necessary for the Son to die for mankind. Such is also the worth of man. Who can now differentiate between the races and the colour of their skin? Can any man or woman be worthless? The value of man cannot be more wondrously expressed than by saying that his Creator died for his redemption.

Adam represented his progeny and failed on their behalf. Christ represented his own, and purchased redemption by his blood. Atonement was the only means of delivering men from the curse of eternal punishment. Man, by contrast, would make himself the author and performer of all that is necessary to secure heaven. The atonement of the Creator for the creature is hard to fathom. Man, by nature, does not understand it. It is foolishness to him (1Cor.1:23,24). Here we may see the wisdom of the Almighty. He alone could solve the dilemma of having to slay the sinner and yet save him. No other being could come up with the answer. By this we may know that God did the impossible to redeem us from hell. "Hereby we perceive the love of God, because he laid down his life for us" (1Jn.3:16). This is God's way. Without it, all will die forever.

Faith is necessary for the application of the atonement to us. It is not mere faith that God exists, but faith in Christ crucified and risen from the dead. Jesus said: "Many will say to me in that day, Lord, Lord, have we not prophesied in your name and in your name have cast out devils and in your name have done many wonderful works? And then I will profess to them, I never knew you, depart from me, you that work iniquity" (Mt.7:22,23). Only those covered by the blood of Christ will be saved, "for there is none other name under heaven given among men, whereby we must be saved" (Acts 4:12).

References

1. Al-Bukhari, vol.6., p.106.
2. Mahmood Shaltoot, Al-Islam, (Beirut,1983), p.129.
3. Al-Bukhari, vol.1, p.28.
4. Ar-Razi's commentary on the *Qur'an*.

Index

Abraham, messengers to, 8
Abrogation, 18-19
ADAM
    fall of, 75-81
    his progeny's involvement in his sin, 81-85
    khalifate of, 67-70
    original nature of, 71-74
    repentance of, 85
Adoptionism, 59-60
'Ali bin abi Taleb, 102-103
    fate of his sons, 103
'Ammar bin Yasir, 24,99
Amorites, 18
ANGEL OF THE LORD, 9-10
Angels, free will of, 70
Anthropomorphism, 16-17
Apocrypha, 55
Arabic language, 22,25,26
ATONEMENT, 142-153
Badr, battle of, 39
Barnabas, gospel of, 56-57
BIBLE
    alleged corruption of, 42-45
    basis of authority of, 5
    canon of, 53-56
    central message of, 11,45
    copyist errors in, 22
    Qur'an's testimony for, 42-43
    unity of, 11
Bukhari al-, 23
CAIN AND ABEL, 125,145
Camel, battle of, 102
CANAANITES
    destruction of, 18
    human sacrifices of, 18
CREATION
    Biblical account of, 20
Cyrus, king of Persia, 49-50
Divorce, 128
EARTH, origin, rotation, shape of, 32-33
Ebionites, 60
Embryology, 35
Gabriel, angel, 6,23,40,62
GARDEN, the, 131-132
Gilgamish, epic of, 5
GOD
    condescension of, 8-9
    his covenant with men, 149-150
    dilemma of, 138,143
    Islamic division of, 134-135

law of, 134-135
nature of, 86-88
repentance of, 17
unity of, 58
GOVERNMENT
civil, 96-111
Christian concept of, 108-110
Qur'anic basis of, 99-102
world, myth of, 97-99
HADITH, the, 7,17,23,24,33, 36,44,62,79,84,92,115,132, 140,145
HEAVEN, 132-133
HEBREW, language, 22
computation of numbers, 22
computation of time, 21
Hell, 132-133
Imputation, 83-84,139,151
Incarnation, 10-11,61-62
INTERPRETATION
principles of, 14-28
Islamic mythology in, 23,68
parallel passages in, 19-20
Intolerance, 1-3,142
JACOB, named Israel, 10
struggle with angel, 9-10
JESUS, the CHRIST
death of, 146-149
deity of, 61-62
earthly kingship of, 108
eternal pre-existence of, 61,64
genealogy of, 20
mankind's blessing, 11-12
mediatorship of, 138-153
sinlessness of, 60, 140
sufficiency of, 46
word of God, 60-61
Jewish people, their plight under the law, 104,105
Jonas, sign of, 21-22
Judgment, final, 130-131
Ka'bah, destruction of, 103-104

Khalid ibn el-Waleed, 99,102
KHALIFATE
comparison with Jewish kingdom, 105-106
struggle for, 102-104
LIBERTY, 112-120
of conscience, 112-114
of faith, 115-120
of speech, 114
LOT, incest of, 19
MAN
fallen nature of, 81-85,89,91
final state of, 129-136
Qur'anic uncertainty, 130
purpose of creation of, 4
MARRIAGE, 126-128
polygamy, 126-128
Mawdudi, Abu el A'la al- author, 101,107
Midrash, the, 44
Mishnah, the, 44
Monotheletes, 2
MUHAMMAD
Biblical prophecy and, 44,47-52
hijra of, 96
illiteracy, 30,45,47
visions, 7
washing heart of, 40
MULTAMIS al- illiterate poet, 31,53
Musailamah the Liar, 31,53
Nicaea, council of, 60
PARAN, 48-49
PROPHETS
alleged sinlessness of, 36-41
QUR'AN
challenge of, 30-32
copyist errors in, 25-27
eternity of, 25
gathering of, 25,27
initial writing of, 22
Muhammad's miracle, 30
science and, 32-35

Resurrection, 129
REVELATION, 4-13
Rida, Muhammad, author, 48,50,51
RITUAL, 23,24
Sabeq, as-Sayyed, author, 48,92,93,118
SEIR, 48-49
Shaltoot, Mahmood, author, 92
SHARI'AH, 133-135
Shi'ites, 23,103
SIN, 86-95
    degrees of, 89-90
    nature of, 86
    state of, 88-89
Sinai, 48-49
SPIRIT, Holy, 50-51,62
    personality of, 52,62
Suyuti al-, 25-27
Talmud, 44
TARAFAH bin al Abd illiterate poet, 31

Theocracy, 104-105
Theophany, 8
THIEVES crucified with Jesus, 20-21
Thomas, gospel of, 23,55
TRADITION, 23-24
    Qur'anic basis of, 24
TRINITY, divine, 58-65
    heathen concept of, 59
    Qur'anic concept of, 59
Uhud, battle of, 18
Universe, expansion of, 32
Unitarianism, 60
USURY, 123-124
Visigothic Arians, 2
WILL, freedom of, 92-94
WINE, 19,121-123
WOMAN, status of in Islam, 126-128,131,132